THE $80 BILLION GAMBLE

THE $80 BILLION GAMBLE

THE INSIDE STORY OF HOW A SUSPICIOUS TICKET, HOT DOGS AND BIGFOOT FOILED THE BIGGEST LOTTERY FRAUD IN U.S. HISTORY

bpc

The $80 Billion Gamble is published by Business Publications Corporation Inc., an Iowa corporation.

ISBN-13 (paperback): 978-1-950790-98-2
ISBN-13 (hardcover): 978-1-950790-90-6
Business Publications Corporation Inc., Des Moines, IA

Business Publications Corporation Inc.
The Depot at Fourth
100 4th Street
Des Moines, Iowa 50309
(515) 288-3336

"EARTH PROVIDES ENOUGH TO SATISFY EVERY MAN'S NEEDS, BUT NOT EVERY MAN'S GREED."

MAHATMA GANDHI

CHAPTERS

FOREWORD

As the Governor of Iowa who signed the law that created the Iowa Lottery in 1985, I found the book, "The $80 Billion Gamble," a fascinating story about how the Iowa Lottery played the key role in foiling the biggest lottery fraud in history.

Though I had misgivings about a state lottery based on the history of fraud and corruption associated with lotteries throughout American history, it became obvious to me that the vast majority of Iowans wanted a state lottery.

At my insistence, the law establishing the lottery has many safeguards against fraud and corruption. These included not employing anyone with a criminal conviction and prohibiting employees and their family members from playing the lottery. The law required transparency and assistance to people with gambling addictions.

This book tells the inside story about how this scheme was exposed and how it led to discovering the successful fraud that Eddie Tipton had accomplished on other lotteries in Wisconsin, Kansas, Colorado, Oklahoma, and other states. The credibility of the $80 billion U.S. lottery industry was riding on solving those cases.

Terry Branstad
U.S. Ambassador to China and Former Governor of Iowa

ACKNOWLEDGEMENTS

The desire to do the right thing is a complex feeling. This book needed to be written to document a mysterious, appalling fraud against multiple U.S. lotteries because history demands a full detailing of the biggest and most colorful case of cheating the industry had ever seen. Even at a time when many in the industry – both those who were scammed by Eddie Tipton and those whose dogged work exposed his crimes – would like to move on to happier thoughts.

We would especially like to thank Mary Neubauer, the Iowa Lottery's vice president for external relations and Rob Porter, Iowa Lottery vice president/general counsel, for their invaluable help in providing documents and other materials and in fact-checking and proofreading. Also, elected and appointed officials, in cluding th e st aff of the att orney general's office, the Iowa DCI, the Iowa Lottery staff, national news media, the compliance group at Scientific Games, Inc, and the directors of many state lotteries who provided records and the support needed to solve this case.

Our thanks to the publishing team at WriteBrain, a division of Business Publications Corp., who helped research and assemble this book to make sure this message gets out: oversight and control are extremely important to the integrity of today's businesses.

And finally, thanks to our families and friends who endured the time and effort it took us to wrestle with the legalities and oversight of dealing with a major fraud against an industry that regularly affects millions of Americans – even those who don't buy lottery tickets – and with the work of weaving this case into what we hope you'll find is a read that is both compelling and important.

Authors, Perry Beeman and Terry Rich

INTRODUCTION

In December 2010, a man bought a Hot Lotto ticket at a convenience store on Des Moines, Iowa's north side. That ticket went on to win the multi-million-dollar jackpot on the line in the Hot Lotto drawing on December 29, 2010. For nearly a year, the prize went unclaimed.

Then, with less than two hours to go before the prize would have expired on December 29, 2011, the winning ticket was presented by lawyers on behalf of a New York investment trust that had been established to benefit a corporation in the country of Belize.

Neither the two lawyers who presented the ticket nor anyone associated with Hexham Investments Trust of Bedford, New York would provide the basic details necessary to verify that the ticket had been legally purchased, legally possessed, and legally presented. Those involved said they could not identify the jackpot winner or the man who purchased the winning ticket.

That standard information is routinely requested from jackpot winners in Iowa as part of the lottery's security processes to comply with both state law and lottery game rules. Such details are usually received within minutes of the time a winning ticket is presented.

On January 26, 2012, Crawford Shaw, a New York attorney who identified himself as the trustee of Hexham Investments Trust, withdrew the claim to the jackpot. That same day, the Iowa Attorney General's Office and Iowa Division of Criminal Investigation opened a criminal investigation into the matter at the request of the Iowa Lottery.

In 2017, three men with Texas ties all pleaded guilty to felony charges in the case, admitting that they conspired to illegally claim lottery winnings by utilizing malicious computer code to rig lottery drawings in five states.

From lottery employees, state staff, attorneys, conspirators, and accomplices, this is a complicated tale full of complex characters and unlikely suspects. The cast of characters is outlined for reference in the back of the book on page 184.

one
A FRAUD UNCOVERED

The trail leading to the undisclosed winner of a $16.5 million Hot Lotto jackpot in Iowa—and the roots of the biggest lottery fraud in U.S. history—warmed considerably when Cassie Kibling routinely answered a phone call in the Iowa Lottery's validation department in early November 2011.

A guy from Waterloo, Iowa, had recently won a Hot Lotto jackpot with a quick pick, meaning he let the lottery terminal pick his numbers randomly. Kibling and colleague Michael Conroy walked to the office door of lottery Vice President Mary Neubauer and said they had just heard from a Hot Lotto winner. Neubauer thought they were talking about the Waterloo ticket. But they weren't.

"No, the OTHER Hot Lotto ticket," one of them said, the one attached to a $16.5 million jackpot.

This was big news. Whoever won that jackpot had not turned in the ticket, even though months had passed.

"That was the ticket that had been out there for 11 months by that point," Neubauer recalled in a video interview recorded for the Iowa Lottery's archives. "We had put out reminder after reminder after reminder looking for that winner. The prize had been won in December 2010."

IOWA LOTTERY

PLAY MEGA MILLIONS! FRIDAYS
ESTIMATED JACKPOT $168 MILLION!
For current drawing results call
Des Moines(515)323-4633

Term:181664   740864
43750028503   12/29/10   20101223 15:24
$16,500.0 $10.00 - 5 Draws
                                12/25/10 - 01/08/11
CASH

Sizzler: NO

A 03 12 16 26 33 Hotball: 11
B 03 12 16 25 35 Hotball: 11

Overall odds of winning are 1:16
Sign it It's yours! All tickets must be signed
before they can be checked or cashed.
Powerball Jackpot $46 Million
Mega Million Jackpot $168 Million

December 29th, 2010 – Actual Hot Lotto jackpot winning ticket. Source: Iowa Lottery

---

After some general questions about how to claim the prize, the caller told Kibling and Conroy he had the ticket. "I think I'm the Hot Lotto jackpot winner," the man said.

The self-proclaimed winner figured it would be simple: "I'll mail you the ticket, you send me the money." That sort of thing.

No muss. No fuss. No names.

The no-names part was a problem, however.

Neubauer took her two colleagues to the lottery security director's office because extra procedures would need to be involved to check the ticket and the background details involved after all that time. She wanted to record the next phone call with the man who claimed to be the winner.

Neubauer got his voicemail when she called the number the man had left. That night, he called back. It was Philip Johnston calling from Quebec. He was a lawyer who later would reveal he operated out of the Turks and Caicos in the Caribbean Sea and represented a clientele that, by his own description, "weren't ALL drug dealers."

He told Neubauer he was the winner of the Hot Lotto prize.

It was a case that would eventually go on a tour of Belize, New York, Colorado, Kansas, Iowa, Oklahoma, Texas, and Wisconsin. And now Canada was in the mix.

Neubauer, a former reporter for the Associated Press, went into investigative mode.

"What brought you to Des Moines when you bought that ticket?" Neubauer asked the man from Quebec.

"It was business, actually," Johnston replied.

The Iowa Lottery's security director and vice president, Steve Bogle, suggested Neubauer ask the man for the Hot Lotto ticket's 15-digit ID number. "It would be almost impossible for someone to just make up 15 digits and get it right," Neubauer said.

Neubauer asked Johnston for the number. Johnston read it to her. "I asked a few more questions, and he was already asking at that time if he actually had to come to Iowa to claim the prize," Neubauer said. She said yes, but she would confirm that.

The ID number checked out, security officials confirmed. Neubauer knew Johnston at least had access to the winning ticket. "We were just going to wait to see where the rest of the story went," she said.

One of the strangest cases in a quarter century of the Iowa Lottery was about to unfold.

Neubauer called Johnston back the next day from Iowa Lottery headquarters. Johnston didn't know it, but Neubauer and others already had watched video footage of the moment the ticket was purchased at a north Des Moines convenience store.

"Do you happen to remember what you wore the day you bought the ticket?" Neubauer asked Johnston. The video showed a heavyset gentleman who appeared to be wearing a black hoodie and jeans.

What happened next will be burned in Neubauer's mind forever.

"He gave a very detailed description of clothing he was wearing that day that was nothing like what we could see on the video. He said he was wearing a suit jacket or blazer and he went into a very detailed description of flannel dress pants. Gray flannel dress pants. I let him give his description," Neubauer said.

Johnston had lied, and Neubauer knew it. "It was clear this wasn't the right information. It was clear this person was up to something," she said.

Or maybe several people were up to something.

Could someone be so stupid as to not realize video cameras record these ticket purchases? Was there some other explanation for the false statement?

Neubauer wanted to let Johnston know that she wasn't buying his bull excrement.

"Huh," she deadpanned over the phone. "Because that sounds nothing like the person we can see in the security camera footage buying the ticket."

That must have made Johnston tip a bit in his lawyerly dress shoes.

Silence followed. Then, "He went on speaking as if I hadn't said anything," Neubauer recalled.

You could imagine Johnston running an index finger along the neck of his shirt as his blazer quickly heated up. The semiformal dress attire he described was nowhere to be seen in the video from the Des Moines convenience store.

"That really annoyed me," Neubauer said, of Johnston's lie, recalling the moment in an interview.

Neubauer was shocked that Johnston didn't take her doubting comment as a chance to admit he had lied.

"Buddy, I was trying to give you a break there by putting you on notice that we have some idea of who was involved in this situation, and clearly your story doesn't match up, and you might want to think about that," Neubauer recalled in an interview. You know, because fraud is frowned upon in the sensible Midwest and in, like, every other part of the country. Some prosecutors see it as a felony. Felony, you know, is a big deal.

"He just kept going like it was inconsequential. So we knew something was wrong," Neubauer added.

Iowa Lottery President and CEO Terry Rich wasn't even in the country when this happened. He was on a cruise, most likely near Belize, he said.

"I get a call," Rich recalled. "Mary is all excited and she's wanting to talk forever and I'm thinking, this is costing us an arm and a leg—more than the cruise costs.

"She says, 'We've got a problem,'" Rich recalled.

Neubauer explained the intricate details of the wardrobe choices of the Canadian lawyer, Johnston, versus the man in the video who bought a ticket with multiple Hot Lotto plays and a couple of hot dogs. That man turned out to be Eddie Tipton of suburban Des Moines. More about him later.

"We don't think we should pay," Neubauer told her suntanned boss.

Rich agreed. "A felony had occurred. If he came in, we would have him arrested on the spot for fraud [under Iowa law]," Rich said.

"We decided we would do the right thing. Ultimately, it would have been easier to deny a claim, let it go to court, and let the court decide, in my opinion, than to pay it and try to go get it [later]," Rich said. "We were ready for this guy."

Bogle recalled that the staff was just trying to find the ticket holder. They were hoping the prize would be claimed. He had met Tipton, who was a security guy and information technology guru at the Multi-State Lottery Association, or MUSL, an organization originally formed by seven states, including Iowa, in 1987 to pool money for bigger prizes. Tipton was going to be visiting the Iowa Lottery staff to make sure they were following MUSL rules—quite ironic, as all would later reflect.

"We got [Johnston] on the phone and he was able to give the serial number off the ticket," Bogle said. "That certainly made my radar antennas go up. That meant he had the ticket or certainly had access to the ticket. Just the nature of the phone call, and the way he talked about things...Having seen and heard the video of the person who actually purchased the ticket, I knew he wasn't the person. This gentleman sounded older. It turned out he was in his 70s. He's from Canada. He didn't have a strong Canadian accent but you knew it was not the same person who bought the ticket.

"That made me think, 'Do we have an insider threat here?'" Bogle recalled. "Do we have someone from the lottery, do we have someone from Scientific Games who was our vendor for running our on-line games, do we have somebody at MUSL? I mean I remember telling people, 'Everybody is a suspect now, even me.'"

And when Neubauer asked about Johnston's clothing, "It was painfully obvious he was not the person who bought the ticket," Bogle said.

During their follow-up call on November 10, 2011, Neubauer asked Johnston if it was his ticket or if he was representing a winner or winners.

"It's my ticket," Johnston said, inaccurately. "It's my ticket. The basic situation, in a nutshell, is I had some business—it's a crazy story." Neubauer laughs. "No, it really is. I had some business interests with some people in Des Moines. I had only been to Des Moines once before. You've got to remember I'm 69 years old, and I'm semi-retired. I'm not an active, practicing attorney. I do security work and I do a lot of consulting work with people, a couple of attorneys in Houston in particular." And a few in New York. Old people, he said.

Someone needed to go to Iowa. "I don't have the ticket yet, but it's on its way," Johnston said with a chuckle. Neubauer also laughed, probably wondering when this semi-retired lawyer, whose Iowa experience spanned one previous trip, would make his second sojourn to Iowa's largest city.

Johnston said his second trip to Iowa was on December 23, 2010. "One of the people said, 'Hey, look there is a lottery coming up, we better do this and invest in this.' I had no idea what they were talking about."

His clients prodded him to join the fun, he said. "They bought a number of tickets, and I got one, which I lodged with an attorney I do business with in Houston," Johnston explained, spinning a yarn. "I forgot all about it."

Neubauer sat in silence, likely trying not to gasp.

"Hello?" Johnston said.

"No, yeah, I'm sorry, we're listening," Neubauer assured him.

Oh, yes, they were listening. Usually tales this big come from a rack of paperback novels, next to the ones with pictures of male models who all look like Fabio.

"SELFISHNESS AND GREED, INDIVIDUAL OR NATIONAL, CAUSE MOST OF OUR TROUBLES."
-PRESIDENT HARRY S. TRUMAN

"I forgot all about it until a couple of months ago and then these numbers came up. It wasn't like I, I, I do business in Des Moines or invest in your lottery, uh, regularly, you know," Johnston said.

Neubauer asked again if Johnston bought the ticket. "No, I bought the ticket…I don't have the ticket yet, but it's coming to me," he said.

"As you said, it's kind of an unusual story," Neubauer replied. "Why don't you have the ticket at your home? Why did you leave it with somebody else?"

Because he left it with his attorney, Johnston responded. Good call. The "call my attorney" defense is popular.

"That's how the whole thing happened," said Johnston, still writing on the fly. "What I would like to do—I don't know if this is possible—I had a heart valve operation about a year ago, up here in Canada, and I don't travel very much." He said he'd like an attorney to claim the ticket and to do the paperwork. He said he would send a copy of the ticket, his passport, and a claim form. He had found Davis Brown, a prominent Des Moines law firm, on the internet. He thought maybe they could help.

Neubauer, composing herself admirably, replied, "I have concerns on several levels," by which she undoubtedly meant, "Holy shit!"

"Those in the room with me do as well. Let me just talk this through with you," Neubauer said.

"Sure," Johnston said. Helpful chap.

At this point, Neubauer knew Johnston was lying, and there would be problems with this win no matter what. The fraud that would frame this case for years had been established, but there were more frauds where that came from.

Neubauer mentioned to Johnston that the ticket would expire on December 29 and had been unclaimed for nearly 11 months. Neubauer spoke of the "significant media coverage" of the big unclaimed prize, including CNN and ABC national reports.

"We are fielding calls from around the world," Neubauer noted. A whole bunch of people claimed to be the winner, but this was the first Canadian attorney who made an impulse lottery ticket buy on a trip to Des Moines in a state known for the blockbuster movie, "Field of Dreams."

Johnston was *dreaming* all right.

Neubauer continued: "You seem to have more details than some of the others who have contacted us, but from a public-perception situation, there is going to be so much attention and so much suspicion surrounding this particular situation, that—while we are always dotting our i's and crossing our t's and following strict security protocols when it comes to our games—in this particular situation, we are going to be going the extra mile because it is so unusual.

"We have never experienced a situation like this in the 26-year history of the Iowa Lottery," Neubauer said.

"That is on top of [the fact that] you're from Canada. I'm sure you are very well familiar with the problems that have been experienced by the Canadian lotteries over the past few years that have received intense public scrutiny up there, including some issues focusing on Lotto Quebec," she added.

"All of that combined means that we are going to have an even higher threshold on this situation that we normally would," Neubauer said.

Johnston appeared unfazed. "That's fine, I don't care about that. If you have the ticket, you have the ticket," he said.

One of Neubauer's colleagues stressed that Johnston would have to present the ticket in person. That is Iowa law.

Then Neubauer spoke of the news interest in the case again.

"We just know how careful we have to be with this particular prize because when it is claimed, it is going to be not only statewide but probably national news because it's such a big prize and it's been unclaimed for so long."

Johnston remained calm and matter-of-fact, especially for a guy who was so obviously lying through his teeth. "I see. Well, if that's the case, that's the case," he said. "I was hoping to do it an easier way."

Neubauer again mentioned the Iowa Lottery's hope that the prize would be awarded...to someone who won it legally. "We are thrilled to hear from you because we have been so afraid that this prize was going to go unclaimed, which is a horrible thing to happen to the prize and to everybody involved, but we do need to be extremely careful."

Johnston asked what he needed to present. Neubauer said it was simple: a claim form, the ticket, himself, and an ID.

"Would it help you if I send in a copy of the ticket ahead of time?" Johnston asked.

"Sure," Neubauer responded.

Johnston said he would send in the claim form, his Canadian Social Security number, and a copy of his passport to help keep things moving.

Neubauer had another question, following up on Johnston's earlier statement that he had only learned he won the jackpot a couple of months earlier.

"I'm just curious, because this whole thing has been such a weird situation, and it continues to be right up to now. How did you find out a couple of months ago that you won?"

Johnston chuckled, softly. "Simply because it hadn't been on my mind, and this thing was an afterthought when I was there on business, and it was an attorney I do business with in Houston that called me and told me."

"Because he had seen the information," Neubauer responded.

"He gave me the numbers," Johnston said. "He says, 'Johnston, I think you won!'"

"That's great," said Neubauer, playing it cool. But questions were swirling in her head about information her lawyer colleagues had helped her compile.

Johnston seemed to suggest he wouldn't want to make a big, public fuss about the win. "I don't intend to make a big statement, believe me." Why go before the Dreaded Media when you know your whole story is baloney, right?

Neubauer then tried to steer Johnston back to reality. She said if she had won $16.5 million, she would have claimed it quickly.

But he said it was because he wasn't in a panic. "I'm not poor, let's put it that way." Not even in Canadian dollars, we guess.

"It's not a big deal, really, to me, in a sense." He said he's used to winning small prizes in Canada's lotteries. No big deal.

Johnston noted his recent heart surgery. He said he had told himself that if he won big he would give "substantial money" to a heart institute in Quebec.

"Guess what? They are going to get a very good if not total portion of this," he said.

Neubauer played along. "Wow! That's fabulous!"

"I don't get too excited because I don't need the money," said Johnston, still trying to explain why $16.5 million didn't prompt action earlier. "I'm not going to do anything with it. I'm not going to buy a yacht. I'm not going to buy a jet plane. I'm 69 years old."

He apparently also wasn't going to buy a big house in Norwalk, Iowa either. But Eddie Tipton, the man who actually bought the winning ticket, would.

Neubauer, working ever more closely to an Academy Award for her role as "Innocent Questioner," said, "Oh, come on, you can live the high-roller life! I'm kidding.

"This whole circumstance just makes me laugh. It's so funny," said Neubauer, not laughing and sounding eager to get to the next question.

She asked again if he bought the ticket in the Des Moines store. "Yeah!" Johnston replied.

Johnston checked his notes. He volunteered that he bought the ticket on December 23, 2010, at 15:24 hours. "I guess that means something."

That's when Neubauer asked that clothing question that eventually made lottery history. Here's your chance to hear Johnston's version from the recorded phone call.

"Hey, do you remember what you were wearing?" she asked Johnston.

"No, honestly not. But I always have either a suit on or a blue sports jacket with gray flannel pants," he replied.

The Case of the Unclaimed Hot Lotto Jackpot was about to take a huge turn.

"OK, all right," Neubauer said on the phone. "It's just that we've seen the videotape from the store and that doesn't sound like the person who bought the ticket."

With just a hint of resignation in his voice, Johnston said, "Well, that's what I had on."

But he may have realized he needed some cover. "I think. I'm not sure."

"When do you think you want to come down?" Neubauer asked.

"Probably early December, but I can't let it go too long, right?"

"The expiration date is 4 p.m. on December 29," Neubauer noted. She repeated how glad lottery officials were to discover the prize would be claimed. The call had lasted 22 minutes, but the one sentence about his attire was frozen in time.

two
THE 'FIB' THAT CHANGED EVERYTHING

On December 5, Neubauer called Johnston, got his voice mail, and told him the package of documentation he had promised never arrived. Bogle was listening to this conversation, and all others, with Johnston.

Johnston called Neubauer back the next day and dropped a bombshell.

"I fibbed. I wasn't the person to buy the ticket," Johnston said. "I was just trying to claim the ticket on behalf of someone who wants to remain anonymous." Others would be in contact, he said. Crawford Shaw, a New York attorney called at one point, and said a Des Moines firm would be in contact.

"The reason I didn't call you back is I've been doing some research on the best way to claim this thing, OK?" Johnston began.

So far, so good. But not for long.

"I've got to tell you the problem all along has been, I told you I'm a lawyer—I told you all this—and I have a client who actually is the one who picked up the ticket and won the lottery," Johnston continued.

Neubauer was not wearing a heart monitor or a blood pressure cuff during this call, but the readings would have been interesting.

"But he has instructed me, and continues to instruct me, [that he is] never to be identified."

Neubauer: "That's, that's…" She couldn't complete a sentence.

Mary Neubauer, Iowa Lottery's VP of External Relations. Source: Iowa Lottery

She had just witnessed confirmation of fraud.

Johnston continued. "We went through all kinds of ramifications on how we could do this initially, then I say, 'Well, call the Iowa Lottery.' I called you. We went through that whole exercise. After we talked, I called him and I said, 'Look, I am not prepared to say that I won the thing because I didn't really win it. You can give me the ticket and maybe I won it, technically, but I'm just not prepared to do that, OK?'"

Neubauer (blood pressure unknown): "OK..." Her head was spinning.

"He said, 'Well, you better find a solution, or we'll just forfeit the thing.' And I said, 'That is crazy.' And he says, 'Well, it's not your decision, is it?' He's a client of mine, OK?"

Neubauer (sounding steady): "Right. Right." Still spinning.

"Everything else I told you is true," Johnston said.

Neubauer, who as a former journalist has a well-honed "b.s." meter, was seething now.

"Unfortunately, I gave you a little fib there," Johnston said. "But I was caught off guard there. I really was just looking for information from you initially."

In October 2016, National Public Radio carried a story headlined, "How Small Fibs Lead to Big Lies." The article explored research by University College London and Duke University, published in Nature Neuroscience. The paper's conclusions included this: "Many dishonest acts are speculatively traced back to a sequence of smaller transgressions that gradually escalated. From financial fraud to plagiarism, online scams and scientific misconduct, deceivers retrospectively describe how minor dishonest decisions snowballed into significant ones over time. Despite the dramatic impact of these acts on economics, policy, and education, we do not have a clear understanding of how and why small transgressions may gradually lead to larger ones."

...a small act, say, like checking to see if you could insert a code to alter lottery drawings just to see if you could do it...and a large act, like, say, committing the largest lottery fraud in U.S. history by manipulating drawings in multiple states...

"I AM A GREEDY, SELFISH BASTARD. I WANT THE FACT THAT I EXISTED TO MEAN SOMETHING.

-THE LATE SINGER, HARRY CHAPIN

Johnston assured Neubauer that he had a plan, and all was well. He was working with Davis Brown, the Des Moines law firm, regarding how to redeem the ticket. And he spoke to Crawford Shaw, a lawyer in New York with whom he had done business.

"So we said, 'What is the procedure we could come up with?' Could we, for instance, set up a revocable trust with the beneficiary being the corporation that I think I alluded to in our first conversation?" Johnston said.

He said he wanted to use a corporation all along, but he didn't think about a trust.

Neubauer mentioned that to her knowledge only publicly named individuals could claim a prize in Iowa, trust or no trust. "There have been trusts formed before to claim a prize, but to the best of my knowledge...a third-party trustee has never been the person to claim the prize," Neubauer told Johnston.

"The difficulty with the situation you are discussing has to do with the piece of Iowa Code that specifies that lottery winners' information MUST be public in Iowa," Neubauer said. "And granted, the laws are different from state to state. And they are certainly much different in your country than they are here."

Neubauer then explained that the Iowa law was intended to prevent fraud—to guard against some crook trying to cheat the money-filled system.

"Folks have been concerned from the very beginning of the lottery about organized crime or ne'er-do-wells trying to hide their income in that fashion," Neubauer said. She didn't say where lawyers representing drug dealers from the Caribbean fit in with those concerns.

Johnston offered a bit more information about the Mystery Winner. "This person does business all over the world...The ticket is legitimate, he just doesn't want his name disclosed," he said.

Johnston said he had told his client he isn't a "magician." He couldn't necessarily make all the ticket holder's wishes appear.

In the latest conversation with Neubauer, Johnston said the clock clearly was ticking on the claim, which would be discarded if a solution that kept the Mystery Winner's identity a secret couldn't be negotiated. Johnston had arranged for his New York lawyer friend to be trustee of a revocable trust. The beneficiary would be a corporation. The trustee would claim the ticket in Des Moines and face the press.

Neubauer said she couldn't say if that would work. She said she understood Johnston's client wanted to remain anonymous.

"He WILL remain anonymous," Johnston insisted.

"Everything you are talking about is probably just going to make it worse," said Neubauer. "From a media curiosity perspective, if someone goes to this great length and tries to put in place all this blind trust information, from a PR and media perspective, you are probably just going to make The Media that much more ravenous for the information about what's really going on here."

And, of course, Neubauer had a point. Reporters can get ravenous—especially when there is free food at the newsroom dining desk—but they are especially aggressive when they think someone is trying to hide something the public has a right to know.

Neubauer had made the point in two separate conversations with Johnston: The Iowa Code requires the winner's identity be made public, whether the person hauled garbage in Rock Rapids, was a college professor in Waverly, or toiled as an I.T. wizard in Des Moines.

Johnston assured Neubauer that everything about this case was legal—another falsehood, as it turned out. It's just that his client didn't even want to be named. We assume he didn't want to discuss his hot dog-eating habits, either.

"Is there anything wrong in that, if the client doesn't want to disclose, and you set up a trust?" Johnston asked Neubauer. "What is wrong with that? I'm a lawyer, this other person is a lawyer, we'd have the trustee. We have the winning ticket. It hasn't been stolen. There isn't anything illegal about that," Johnston explained.

So that ruled out, at least in Johnston's mind, one of the things that could go wrong with a ticket.

But what about the other possibilities?

✔ It was taken by a crooked convenience store clerk.

✔ It's mutilated.

✔ It was claimed by someone who insisted on anonymity in Iowa, where state law doesn't allow that.

✔ It was claimed by someone who insisted on anonymity, was barred from buying lottery tickets in Iowa because of direct professional ties to the lottery industry, and had tampered with the system to work around very long odds. Iowa law doesn't allow that, either.

Neubauer and Bogle said they'd have to check with the Iowa Attorney General's Office.

In the meantime, Johnston, who had earlier said he had bought the ticket and described the clothes he was wearing, now told Neubauer he didn't buy the ticket, wasn't the man on the camera, and wasn't in Des Moines the day the ticket was purchased.

"I'm not going to lie," Johnston told his client after learning that the Iowa Lottery had video of the person who bought the ticket. "I told him, 'I'm a lawyer for God's sake. Lawyers have a bad enough reputation as it is.' I am not going to lie—I've already lied, I think."

Lawyers' rank in the public esteem has been a subject of steady debate and ratings. A 2017 Gallup Poll list of professions Americans considered the most honest and ethical found that nurses topped those ranked "high" or "very high."

Newspaper reporters came in 13th and TV reporters 15th. Lawyers ranked 17th, above business executives, advertising practitioners, and members of Congress. Public relations workers didn't make the top 20.

Neubauer, back on the call, probably had the word "liar" ringing in her ears. But she kept cool and professional.

"I compliment you for calling me today and sharing this information because we already knew it wasn't you," Neubauer said. "It clearly wasn't you."

Johnston then thought his brand, or at least his reputation, could use some triage.

"I'm not a bad guy," Johnston said later as he described trying to find a legal way for his client to claim a prize that was the result of illegal doctoring of lottery computers. And his "client," it turned out, couldn't legally play the lottery.

Neubauer tried to bear down on the truth. She wanted the truth. She could handle the truth.

"You have said you are representing a client. Is your client the individual who went into the store and purchased the ticket?" Neubauer asked Johnston.

"Yep," Johnston replied. "Yep."

"Ok. He personally purchased that ticket?" Neubauer asked, for confirmation.

"I believe so, yeah. That's my information," Johnston replied.

Neubauer said she would check on a few things and call him back.

"Just tell me exactly what we can or can't do," Johnston said. "I'm sorry I misled you a little bit. I was kind of forced to do that. I didn't feel comfortable with it."

Rich recalled that it was about this time that Iowa investigators kept information restricted to four or five members of the team in case the suspicious case of the unclaimed ticket was an inside job of some sort, but at this point, they had little reason to think it was.

In her own call with Johnston, Molly Juffernbruch, the Iowa Lottery's general counsel in 2010, said that Johnston's client would need to come in for an interview with security officials to get the prize. "If you wanted to try to collect as a trust that would be fine, but we at the lottery would need a name." The name of the person who bought the ticket and would redeem the prize.

Of course, this case had already become a bit of a circus, and even three rings probably wouldn't be enough for what was coming up. Juffernbruch tried to ease any concern Johnston may have had that the media would get ahold of the situation.

"We could tell you that we aren't going to call in the media and do a media event while your client was here," Juffernbruch offered, unprovoked. "But the name probably would end up being public information, and we would probably have to just announce who the winner was, but we could do that after your client collected the jackpot so they wouldn't be exposed to the all the cameras and such, if that would be a better solution for your client."

She sounded as though the news cameras were the equivalent of chicken pox or measles—something you wouldn't want to be exposed to.

When she paused, Johnston spoke.

"But you have to disclose his name, correct?" Johnston asked. "Yes" was the answer. Juffernbruch mentioned that there had been a lot of interest in the case and some conflicting claims. And, by the way, vendors can't win, she noted. Like people who work for MUSL.

"We need an in-person interview, and we need a name," Juffernbruch concluded.

Johnston, matter-of-factly, said, "No thanks."

"Ok, I am not sure that is going to work in this case, so I'm afraid this particular lottery will go unclaimed."

Juffernbruch appeared more ruffled than had the poker-faced Neubauer.

"You, you, you think it will go unclaimed?" Juffernbruch asked.

"Yes, I'm certain of it," said Johnston, sounding as though he thought he was clear the first time.

"Because we really do like to award the prizes," Juffernbruch responded. She asked if anything could be done.

"I have a client who is refusing for his own personal reasons. I can't disclose what they are—it could be debts, it could be anything—to put their names forward," Johnston said. "I do business with this person. I am in Canada but I do business with him in the states. He's a very difficult person. He doesn't want his name disclosed."

It turns out being "difficult" doesn't get you out of complying with state law according to Iowa Code.

Johnston said he had researched options and talked to the Davis Brown law firm in Des Moines, and to Shaw in New York. "I said, 'Well, maybe they will accept a trust, because other states have done that, and other lotteries have done that. Some have even accepted a blind trust, apparently,'" Johnston said.

But Juffernbruch said that wouldn't work in Iowa, though she repeated her offer to spare Johnston's client the bubonic plague—er, media attention—by allowing "lower publicity levels than we would normally have."

Johnston said his client feared publicity. Clearly.

But a security check was required, Juffernbruch said. Johnston said he understood.

"I can assure you the ticket isn't stolen or anything, but beyond that I wouldn't know," Johnston said.

"I hope you can get your client to reconsider," Juffernbruch said.

"I'm going to try," Johnston replied. "It's a lot of money."

"You can tell him we're nice people," Juffernbruch said, continuing her point that the lottery wanted to award the prize if legally possible.

"I think he already knows that," Johnston replied.

What Johnston called a "fib" in November 2011 opened one of the wildest, most intense—and newsworthy—investigations in U.S. lottery history, Rich said. Johnston had lied to the Iowa Lottery. He committed fraud.

Investigators were primed to solve the case of the Mystery Winner. They found this interesting: Who was the president of the Belize-based trust, Hexham Investments, that Johnston said could claim the prize? Philip Johnston of Quebec.

That set up a later twist, but for now Neubauer had to address the task at hand.

"We were glad to hear that someone had the ticket still, but certainly none of the questions had been answered," she recalled later.

Dozens of others had contacted the lottery claiming to have won the jackpot. Some said they lost the ticket. Others said it was stolen. At least one said it might be in a wrecked car at the junkyard.

"We knew we had our work cut out for us," Neubauer said.

The case went on for months. There were leads from all over the United States. There was this odd tie to Belize.

"This was going to be complicated just to follow the trail in this case," Neubauer said. "We knew it wasn't going to be an easy road." She marveled, in gratitude, that the Iowa Division of Criminal Investigation, the Iowa Attorney General Tom Miller's office, and her Iowa Lottery colleagues stayed the course on the investigation, which lasted for more than three years.

three

OF CHEATING, BAD CHOICES AND A SYSTEM THAT EXPOSED BOTH

To put this case in perspective, it helps to look at other big cases through the years, involving other lotteries. It's good to consider the kind of greed that drives a human being in a situation like this.

The Tipton case certainly wasn't the first attempt at cheating a lottery or casino. Modern-day cases go back to the Triple Six Fix scam against the Pennsylvania 666 game in 1980. In a scam that was laid out in the movie "Lucky Numbers," starring John Travolta and Lisa Kudrow, the host of the lottery drawing show and his accomplices used latex paint to weight some of the balls used in the drawing, reducing possible combinations to eight. They won $1.8 million, most of which was never paid, and the conspirators went to jail after authorities got a tip and noticed unusual betting patterns that warranted investigation.

In another instance, a technician who had worked for a lottery vendor in Pennsylvania in 1988 altered the system to print a duplicate ticket to try to grab a $15.2 million jackpot no one had claimed. He was eventually caught when reviews revealed that the paper wasn't the proper type. The man, Henry Arthur Rich (of no relation to Terry), eventually pleaded guilty.

Between 1993 and 1995, another computer whiz and an accomplice, this time in Nevada, modified slot machines when a certain string of coins were dropped in. They stole thousands before the computer jockey, Ronald Dale Harris, got greedy and tried to bilk Keno machines in Atlantic City. A routine check on a $100,000 jackpot and the straight-faced reaction of his accomplice to the win led authorities to crack the case. Harris was sentenced to seven years in prison.

Then there was the Milan Lotto scam of 1995-1999. In that case, gang members bribed children to squint through blindfolds they wore while picking lottery balls from a spinning drum, telling them to pick the shiniest ones, or the ones that were heated or frozen. Nine people won $174 million before they were caught and arrested after authorities saw suspicious patterns.

But none of those cases was quite like Eddie Tipton's attempt to scam lotteries in at least five states.

His case was an unusual mix of greed, chutzpah, stupidity and technical talent.

Greed weaves through this narrative. One example of this particular greed was the building of a 4,800-square-foot house with a movie theater and gym, set on 22 acres near Des Moines, Iowa.

Mahatma Gandhi, the civil rights leader who led India's independence movement, said, "Earth provides enough to satisfy every man's needs, but not every man's greed."

But greed is a bane of human existence that goes back millennia.

The Qur'an says of greed: "O you who believe, do not nullify your charities by inflicting reproach and insult, like one who spends his money to show off, while disbelieving in God and the Last Day. His example is like a rock covered with a thin layer of soil; as soon as heavy rain falls, it washes off the soil, leaving it a useless rock."

The Bible says in the Gospel of Luke, "Then he said to them, 'Watch out! Be on your guard against all kinds of greed; a man's life does not consist in the abundance of his possessions.'"

The man in the middle of this saga led a comfortable life in Norwalk, a suburb of Des Moines, Iowa—a mid-sized capital city that is far more metropolitan than you may think. Des Moines, a financial center, relies on Midwestern values of honesty, fair play, and hard work to fuel a business climate and quality of life that has landed the city on many lists of the best places to live, raise a family, work, or start a business. Millennials especially love Des Moines; they have said so in surveys. It is surprisingly urban, has a strong vibe of growth, and has a relatively low cost of living. The people are nice, it's true.

The man in this case had the American dream, too, as evidenced in part by that mansion he was building that seemed to some to be beyond his means.

That man—Eddie Tipton—came into some money that would help him achieve his dreams. But he came into the money the wrong way.

Eddie Tipton knew how to program a computer to do what he wanted it to do...even if it wasn't legal...even if he committed a felony doing it.

This is a story about investigators seeking the truth that would set them free, even if it didn't do the same for lottery manipulator Eddie Tipton and his Bigfoot-hunting brother, Tommy. It's about public servants spending hours on what looked like a dead-end case, toiling all along to be transparent.

It's the story of how someone managed to cheat a system that was considered impenetrable, racking up millions of dollars in lottery wins across five states, and how he got caught.

But this isn't just the story of a fixed lottery play.

At its core, it is a deflating tale of *greed*—one that enveloped a middle-aged man and his friends and relatives, not to mention robbing precious hours from an investigator whose son, drawing his first breaths on Earth, had to do without his father way more than he should have in those important, bond-forming moments of early life. That father, Rob Sand—whom you'll meet later in more detail—was busy negotiating the fine points of a case that would prove when systems are in place to catch fraud, they typically work, even if the crime is an inside job.

This is a play-by-play of one of the United States' weirdest and most important lottery-related cases of all. We'll show how a determined band of investigators in Iowa—at times discouraged by their own peers in other states from looking into a case that could expose security weaknesses—

steadfastly pieced the case together. You'll see the investigators, through prodding and pointed questions and careful calling of bluffs, break open the case that for years looked like a nagging dead end.

This saga features a lead character who worked for a national organization that gave him too many "keys to the kingdom"—a man who decided to play even more fixed lottery draws and brazenly and publicly buy tickets himself, even after bagging more money than most would dare think possible. It is the story of people who might have won big in a fair game but didn't. And it's the story of some who won legitimately but had to split the prize with a crook who fixed the game.

The result was more than $2 million in illegally obtained prizes from drawings in five states—and a prison term of up to 25 years for the central figure in the case. That man, hired to secure the very system he violated, defrauded his own employer. The tampering began, he said later, with an offhand comment from a colleague that left the ill-fated lotto winner wondering if he could scam the security system underpinning a massive system of lotteries across the nation. He claimed he initially just wanted to see if it could be done. Later, he decided to cheat the system.

"I want to make one thing perfectly clear," Rich would say later, as he looked back on the case and planned his New Year's Eve 2018 retirement. "We didn't ask for this job. It landed in our laps. It's been unique, it's been tough, it's been mysterious, and a lot of different things. Personally, I came into the job enjoying promotion, marketing, and business, and it looks like I'll end it with ethics—what do you do, with integrity, when something happens."

four
BIG WINS AND CONFETTI

In Iowa, a relatively small state, big jackpots seem to come after long droughts.

The lucky ones in Iowa have included a single mother from Redfield, a tiny town west of Des Moines. Fifty-one-year-old Lerynne West won half of a $687.8 million Powerball jackpot on October 27, 2018 after she left the winning ticket blowing around in her sister's truck. Her cash payment was $198.1 million. She almost immediately announced, on Ellen DeGeneres' talk show, that she would donate $500,000 to the Travis Mills Foundation—a foundation that supports wounded veterans.

West won fair and square. She was altruistic. She knew, as the fictional character George Costanza of "Seinfeld" fame did, that we live in a *society*. She had treated that society better than Eddie Tipton had.

"The Shipping 20" from Cedar Rapids, Iowa were a blue-collar bunch who split $241 million in 2012. It was, at that time, the biggest Iowa prize won in the history of Powerball, a national game run by the Multi-State Lottery Association—Eddie Tipton's employer—based in Clive, Iowa. It was another clean win by people whose lives were changed forever through the simple act of legally buying lottery tickets.

A $202 million Powerball prize in 2012 went to Mary and Brian Lohse, a couple in the Des Moines suburb of Bondurant who paid off their church's mortgage and helped pay for a new football stadium and

November, 2018 – One of the nation's largest Powerball winners, Lerynne West with Iowa Lottery's Mary Neubauer and Terry Rich. Source: Iowa Lottery

grocery store in their community. Brian was elected to the state House of Representatives in November 2018.

But this case in 2011 was unusual.

A corporation in the Central American nation of Belize with ties to New York, Houston, and Canada was ready to claim a $16.5 million Hot Lotto prize, which was "won" against 1 in 10.9 million odds with a ticket purchased by a large, hoodie-wearing man at a Des Moines convenience store.

The man who bought the ticket steadfastly refused to be identified— which in Iowa means you don't get the prize. It is Iowa state law that you must be identified to claim the prize—law designed to keep the mob and other unwholesome elements out of the lottery system.

five
SETTING THE STAGE

Typically, the get-quick-rich experience of buying lottery tickets in the United States has little to do with Bigfoot, cheap hot dogs, face-shielding hoodies, and trusts based in Belize.

In Iowa the drill has become familiar. Many people buy a ticket or two to feel the excitement of "what if." The Lottery's one-time tagline, "You Can't Win If You Don't Play," rings in their ears. They lose or win small. The Iowa Lottery's own staff regularly warns people to play only for fun. Don't expect to win, just be glad if you do, Neubauer regularly counsels.

Inevitably, though, someone beats millions-to-one odds—occasionally even the 1 in 292 million odds of Powerball, one of the marquee lottery games in the United States. Every once in a while, someone manages to win against odds so close to zero many don't even bother to play.

In the biggest single-ticket lottery win in the United States, an unidentified person (as of December 2018) bought a Mega Millions ticket in South Carolina that won a $1.5 billion jackpot in October 2018. A previous Powerball jackpot of $1.6 billion was split among several winners who bought tickets in Munford, Tennessee, at a grocery store in Florida's Melbourne Beach, and in the Los Angeles suburb of Chino Hills in 2016.

Surveillance photo of Eddie Tipton purchasing the winning Hot Lotto ticket in December, 2010. Source: Iowa Lottery

Presumably, those jackpots were won legitimately, by people who either asked the computer to choose the numbers that would be printed on the ticket or submitted their own numbers, perhaps based on anniversary or birth dates or some other meaningful detail of their lives. They got lucky, and that's it.

That turned out to be too big of a chance to take for Eddie Tipton, a Texas native and computer scientist who came to work in Iowa...in the lottery industry.

Tipton is a giant of a man, at least physically. Some say he's a smart guy. But despite working for an interstate association of lotteries, MUSL, he decided to lumber into a Des Moines convenience store with his head wrapped in a hoodie to illegally buy lottery tickets. He also made two of the most infamous hot dog purchases in American convenience-store history.

In the process, he set off the most bizarre, twisting, and potentially costly lottery scandal the United States has ever seen. A cyber-sleuthing team of Iowa-based investigators worked through what happened before Tipton bought those two special lottery tickets at a convenience store on the north edge of Des Moines and eventually solved a dizzying case that oozed suspense, cheating, unintended humor, and, in the end, justice.

six
THE BEGINNING OF A WILD RIDE

Let's look more closely at the Iowa scandal.

The Iowa Lottery holds flashy, celebratory news conferences for big wins. Neubauer and Rich always made sure they were well-dressed for the cameras with wide smiles sporting well-polished, white teeth. Together, the duo presented oversized checks to the winners as confetti rained from the studio ceiling. Onlookers alternated between being happy for the winners and wondering why they couldn't manage to win a couple of bucks, let alone millions.

Rich is a jovial, silver-haired gentleman who made a name for himself in cable television as a promoter and by running the zoo in the Iowa capital of Des Moines. In February 2009, he became CEO of the Iowa Lottery, making him the face of an institution that has funneled $1.9 billion to Iowa's state government services—veteran assistance, education, and parks among them. For nearly a decade before he retired at the end of 2018, Rich was most visible to the public as the guy who joyfully presented millions of dollars to jackpot winners.

Neubauer has been running the public relations operations at the Iowa Lottery since 1999.

Their usual joint announcements about lottery wins were routine, but what happened January 26, 2012 was unexpected and extraordinary.

Rich donned his usual crisp white shirt and dark suit, added a splash of color with a violet tie, and stood before the Des Moines press corps with an announcement on January 26, 2012.

Someone had bought a winning Hot Lotto ticket at a Des Moines convenience store on December 29, 2010 but never claimed the $16.5 million prize—a 1 in 10.9 million win in a truly random drawing. There had been great suspense about the winner, and some inquiries about cashing the ticket, but still no one knew who won the ticket after the man in the hoodie manually submitted what turned out to be the winning numbers, 3, 12, 16, 26, 33, and Hot Ball 11.

"Ladies and gentlemen, the Hot Lotto jackpot claim has been withdrawn," Rich told reporters at the 2012 news conference, his voice full of purpose and his face sporting the hint of a smile he nearly always shows.

Lawyers from Hexham Investment Trust, of Belize, had pulled the prize claim, shocking the public, if not Rich, who had, in effect, called the potential winner's bluff. The lottery was pushing for the name of the ticket purchaser—again, because lottery officials co nsider that a requirement under Iowa law before any prize can be awarded. Eventually, they told the lawyers who had been shielding a mystery winner behind the Belizean trust that they had to identify the person by a certain date, as the lawyers would say. They didn't.

No one with the Iowa Lottery had any clue who the Hot Lotto winner was.

What was happening here? What was the person hiding?

Was the winner too young to legally buy a ticket? Was the winning ticket stolen? Was there reason to believe someone was trying to play the system, as well-protected and secure as it was and still is? Investigators even wondered, among themselves if the winner had met an unfortunate demise after revealing the win to the wrong person.

Rich and his crew knew the integrity of the $80 billion U.S. lottery industry was riding on making sure there was no fraud. The I owa Lottery alone is a $350-million-a-year business that the state depends on for revenue.

Lottery officials were about to be left with a jumbled Rubik's cube of a case. The winner had even offered to give the money to charity—but only if the state would award the prize without divulging who won. The Iowa Lottery team politely declined to break state law by allowing anonymity.

"Something stunk," Rich would later recall in his usual, simple, jargon-free terms.

The masterful ad-libber, Rich uncharacteristically read from a prepared statement late in the news conference. The message was this: The Iowa Division of Criminal Investigation and the Iowa attorney general were called in to make sure there was no fraud in the case.

"The Iowa Lottery Authority recently requested the Iowa Division of Criminal Investigation and the Iowa attorney general investigate the circumstances surrounding the purchase and presentation of a multimillion-dollar winning ticket purchased in December 2010," Rich said. "The DCI and attorney general will continue their investigation in order to ensure the integrity of the lottery and to determine if those involved complied with state law."

That seemed like basic due diligence in a way, and Rich's matter-of-fact tone almost sounded like he didn't expect to find anything. Reporters were immediately skeptical. It was an odd case that had taken them, and the public, for a wild ride, and now some mysterious trust based in Belize had figured in a major lottery win in Des Moines, which was not normally an epicenter of corruption.

Rich tried to make sense of it all at the news conference. His message seemed to be that the system worked.

"The lottery has been around 25 years, and, you know, we can speculate on what legally is good, and it may not work with every prize," Rich said. "It's ours to make our best judgment. That's why we have the procedures; that's why we have the rules.

"I think those rules and the Iowa Code set up through the Legislature and the governor really was a good ending to what could be a different kind of story," Rich told the assembled reporters at the bombshell news conference.

Rich seemed relieved that the prize wasn't awarded, but it was clear they couldn't simply discard the mystery like so many non-winning lottery tickets.

"Really, I think, we could speculate, but we don't need to because obviously this turned out." He raised his open hands for emphasis. "And from my end, we'll move on and continue to give away a lot of money and have a lot of fun with the lottery."

Everything sounded fine, at least by the tone of Rich's voice. The authorities would continue to look at it just in case, but the message seemed to be "go forth and buy lottery tickets. No story here."

But the story was there, and it was only beginning. Rich sensed something wasn't right.

The $80 billion U.S. lottery industry was at risk.

Want to know how much money $80 billion really is? U.S. residents spent $80.39 billion on lottery tickets in 2017, nearly eight times the $11 billion they shelled out for movie tickets. They paid $56 billion to attend sports events. Nothing in the entertainment industry comes close to the magnitude of the combined, dream-fueled purchase of lottery tickets. The ritual of buying a ticket to test the odds, to wonder if life would be changed forever, is quite a thing to behold in all its randomness. Because the winners are chosen at random.

Right?

Veteran Des Moines Register reporter Daniel Finney covered the Iowa Lottery's news conference at lottery headquarters in suburban Des Moines. He didn't hesitate to ask his first question once Rich yielded.

The New York reporters on the phone couldn't hear the chatter in Des Moines, so Rich repeated the inquiry from the Des Moines journalist. "The question was, 'What the hell? What's going on here?'" Rich said. Neubauer laughed, perhaps to take some tension out of the air, or perhaps merely reacting spontaneously to another smooth bit of TV from her boss and mentor, Rich, a TV veteran. Or maybe it was a nervous chuckle.

"From the beginning, we knew this was a unique case," Rich said. "We set up, as we do with every lottery play, certain security protocols we do to be able to award the prize. From the beginning, we had not received the information that we had requested. It has been one of the strangest lottery claims that we've had in the 26-year history of the Iowa Lottery. For our chapter, it brings to a close a very unique and interesting situation."

Again, he sought closure. If only it were that easy.

Rich had relayed to the media, and therefore to the public, that the money would be put up for grabs in future lottery prizes, with each state involved in the Hot Lotto getting its share.

He ended the press conference with a tone that sounded like the case was over, all was fine, and he could go back to grip-and-grin photos with certified, publicly identified winners of lottery prizes.

Then again, his instincts had already told him to keep looking for trouble. Something didn't add up. Was everything truly fine? Was it time to move on?

This was a case that eventually would take the well-traveled Rich and his team on an investigative sojourn, by air and by phone, from Canada to Texas and from Texas to New York.

The case had it all: Bigfoot hunting. A Belizean trust. Computer tampering. Inside jobs. An out-of-state lawyer who felt compelled to try to impress people in a Des Moines bar by bragging about a lottery prize he claimed he had won but hadn't.

The case would introduce Rich, trusted lottery vendor Scientific Games' security group led by former FBI Assistant Director Larry Potts, and Rich's colleagues in Iowa and other states to two brothers in crime. One of the brothers would make an offhand comment about hot dogs that ended up making national news and inadvertently broke a legal case wide open. The Iowa Lottery team would learn more computer science than they cared to know as investigators drilled deep into the chip boards to see if the lotteries of America really were fail-safe.

Strange case, indeed.

seven

THE BASICS OF THE CASE

Native Texan Eddie Tipton got a job at MUSL. After his co-worker suggested, apparently in jest, that Tipton could fix the winning numbers for lottery games, Tipton came up with a computer code, supposedly to see, in an academic sense, if rigging the system was possible. And then he did rig the system...across state lines.

By the time he was through, a weird combination of Bigfoot hunting friends of his brother's, an FBI agent who was tipped off by a comment about a hot dog, a lying lawyer from Canada, and people who recognize Eddie Tipton's voice in security-camera video forced Tipton to make a plea deal calling for him to serve up to 25 years for a series of frauds and tampering with the system. As this book went to print in early 2019, Tipton was still at a medium-security state prison in Clarinda — a city of about 5,300 in southwest Iowa that is the birthplace of jazz great Glenn Miller. Tipton declined to be interviewed for this book but we have his words from court documents and other sources.

In fact, we have a lot of material you've never seen – despite heavy press coverage of this case. We're here to give you the ultimate inside view of what happened—complete with the smoking-gun videos, letters, transcripts, court documents, phone call recordings, bald-faced lies, and live TV appearances.

eight
WHO IS EDDIE TIPTON?

Eddie Raymond Tipton was most often holed up in his bedroom working on computers when his siblings were out working the farm when they were kids, his brother Tommy recalled in a court deposition.

Eddie was a computer guy. Years after those childhood missions, he earned a bachelor's degree in management information systems and finance from the University of Houston.

Well into his professional career, Eddie worked a stint as chief operating officer of Systems Evolution Inc. with his buddy Robert Rhodes as CEO—a tie that will become important later in this story. Tipton was a self-described "single guy" who was making a base salary of $108,580 by the time his work became a topic of legal interest. He worked as a computer scientist at the Multi-State Lottery Association, which is based in a Des Moines suburb. The association facilitates multijurisdictional games, such as the flagship Powerball, and takes care of many of the day-to-day workings of some lottery games, including their drawings.

Tipton started at MUSL (pronounced like the word "muscle"), as the association is known in the lottery business, in 2003. He eventually became frustrated by 50- and 60-hour weeks that included shifts designed to run until 11 p.m. One time while on vacation, Eddie was just getting off a jet ski when he got a frantic call from the office. Eddie was not pleased. His boss, helpfully, reminded him that Eddie was on call 24 hours a day.

At one point, he recommended Jason Maher for the network engineer position at MUSL, and Maher was hired. Tipton and Maher met at Taki restaurant, one of the better sushi places in Des Moines. Tipton and Maher would burn off steam by playing the video game "Clan."

Many days, Tipton seemed like a normal guy going about his business—an "everyman" with computer skills.

But this seemingly normal guy had brushes with the law before he applied at the Multi-State Lottery Association where he would do sensitive computer work.

When he applied at MUSL, Tipton said he only had traffic tickets on his record. An Iowa background check didn't find anything else, and there was no national background check.

But Tipton lied about his record on his application.

Tipton had a couple of entries on his criminal record. One was a burglary that resulted from "hanging out with the wrong crowd," he said during a legal proceeding many years later. "As I recall, they went into a storage unit and it had belonged to their mother, or something like that. And then it just so happened I had been working on fence. I was a country kid working on fence. I had bolt cutters in the back of my truck. They were like, 'Hey, let's use these.' They grabbed the bolt cutters and took them and started cutting locks on storage units. I got in trouble for that."

Tipton also had a theft case, which he recalled as more of an argument with a Sears employee over software. "It was Jerry Springer style," Tipton said. He referred to the former politician-turned TV talk show host whose set was known for being filled with fights that resulted from Springer's efforts to ignite trouble among guests. Once the fight broke out, often among women trying not to lose their clothes, Springer's crew of bouncers would make purposely weak efforts to break up the altercations while the cameras recorded the action and the ratings soared.

"They decided to charge me with theft," Tipton recalled in an interview with investigators. He later testified that there may have been something about disturbing the peace. Or shoplifting. He couldn't remember exactly.

Whatever the charges were, Tipton claimed he fessed up to them before he interviewed for the job at MUSL, where he would eventually take his criminal record to a whole new level.

During legal proceedings, Tipton confirmed that within a year of joining MUSL, Tipton had responded to that off-hand comment from a colleague asking him what the winning numbers would be and suggesting Tipton could set them.

Investigators would learn later that Tipton installed the malicious computer language as computers were built, as early as 2004. Within a year after that fateful talk with the colleague about tampering with the system, Tipton had rigged a jackpot in Colorado and a friend of his brother claimed the prize through a trust. A few years later, in 2007, he did the same in Wisconsin and a business friend claimed that jackpot.

He also rigged a 17-state jackpot play in Iowa and two small jackpots in Kansas. He had set up the computers so they would produce a single predictable draw a year, at best. Tipton claimed in his interview with investigators that he didn't always win on the dates he chose for altered drawings.

When Tipton fumbled the claiming of the Iowa jackpot, he arranged a final 17-state Hot Lotto win in Oklahoma before realizing his secret was going to come out, and he was likely in serious legal trouble.

Tipton had installed a code that narrowed the possible combinations and set certain dates and conditions, under which he would know what numbers could be in play. Even his doctored odds were complicated by the fact that lottery officials flipped a coin to decide which random-number generator—which computer—would be used for that drawing.

The saga involved lottery scams in Colorado, Wisconsin, Iowa, Kansas, and Oklahoma, in that order. We'll take you through the details state by state. The cases had two critical things in common: Eddie Tipton and his cheating code.

nine
FIRST STOP: THE COLORADO LOTTERY

The best way to chronicle the frauds committed by Tipton and his friends is to work through them in the order they happened.

Tipton told Iowa state investigator Rob Sand that his original fraud-aided win, in Colorado, came after he decided to have his brother, Tommy, make a play. It was 2005, five years before he unsuccessfully sought to scam Iowa for the biggest prize he sought.

"To the best of my memory, my brother was going on a trip and I suggested that I had some numbers that he could play. And that was pretty much it," Eddie Tipton told Sand.

Tipton knew that his brother would be traveling on one of the three dates on which he had rigged the computers to narrow the field of possible winning combinations to perhaps 200.

Tipton had written down approximately 200 number combinations on a "big yellow pad" and gave them to his brother, Tommy. He didn't want to leave anything to chance.

"If you want a chance to win you need to play all of these," Eddie told Tommy. "I don't know if any of them will win, but you're going anyway. But these have a good chance of winning based on my analysis."

You would think Tipton might have checked the results of the Colorado Lottery on the date he had set for one of his predetermined wins, but he claimed he didn't.

Iowa Assistant Attorney General and Prosecutor Rob Sand. Source: Rob Sand

"No, I did not," he told Sand. It was Tommy who contacted Eddie to tell him that one of his plays won. Eddie wasn't expecting a payout. "It's pretty much his to do [with] what he wanted," was Eddie's thought.

Eddie claimed he never planned to use the code he installed to win a prize but decided to give the numbers to his brother to see if the software worked. "Technically, it was in three different states and I could have, you know, just hired a whole bunch of people and started playing and just have all these claims, but I didn't do any of that. That was never my intent," Eddie Tipton told Sand.

He wanted to help his brother. That's just the kind of warm-hearted crook he was.

"[Tommy's] got five daughters, he had kids going to college. I knew he needed it…At the time he was constantly having issues with his wife," Eddie Tipton said.

And what man whose wife gets testy on occasion doesn't immediately hope a sibling is a computer jockey who could fix a multimillion dollars lottery to scrape up some cash to soothe the wounds of marital strife?

It turned out, despite his alleged remote interest in the outcome of the numbers, Eddie had visited Colorado before the drawing to make sure the computers were set to the right time, knowing that computer time floats when they aren't connected to the internet. His code wouldn't work if the time was off.

Eddie also said Tommy had agreed to loan him money. He bought land from his boss, Ed Stefan, the man who hired Eddie in 2003. Eddie built a $540,000 house next to Stefan's large house. Eddie would borrow the jackpot money until his house was sold, Tommy testified. Eddie eventually sold the house for $590,000 in July 2015 as his legal problems mounted.

Alexander Hicks, a friend of Tommy's from Texas, claimed a share of the $4.5 million jackpot because Tommy didn't want to. Besides having a general fondness for money, Hicks, now deceased, and Tommy Tipton had something else in common: they both hunted Bigfoot, the legendary—some would say imaginary—giant creature of folklore.

For all of Eddie Tipton's gyrations before the draw—with at least some idea that the numbers he listed on sheets from a yellow legal pad he shared with his brother would win—two others also won in that same jackpot drawing. One was believed to be Tommy's lawyer, who, it turned out, copied the numbers from the pad Tommy showed him and took much of his crooked client's money. The other winner was someone who let the lottery terminal pick the numbers printed on his ticket, as so many people do.

Eddie Tipton and his brother didn't let the computer choose their numbers. They had Eddie's can't-miss numbers, which needed to be written on the lottery ticket forms by hand.

ten
BIGFOOT

Eddie Tipton's brother, Tommy, was a justice of the peace in Texas.

He also hunted Bigfoot.

Somehow, the juxtaposition isn't as jarring as one might expect given the territory involved. Texans like their hunting. However, History.com reports that the Bigfoot legend traces back to a 1958 column in the Humboldt Times newspaper in northern California that had fun with a letter-to-the-editor about big footprints reported by loggers in the area. The legend of the big, hairy, ape-like creature continues to this day.

Tommy Tipton would travel to various states looking for Bigfoot, which he described as a big creature that likes to torment farm animals.

"My grandmother was raised on a farm in Arkansas where this creature would come in and harass all the farm animals," Tommy Boyd Tipton explained in a legal proceeding.

But there was more. His great-grandfather was an eyewitness, too. "My great-grandfather, when he would plow, when this creature would come through the farm, the mules would not in any way go to the opposite end of the field down toward the bottoms."

When Tipton was little, his grandmother would tell stories of a beast that harassed the family. Later, Tipton discovered he could share his stories of intrigue on the internet. Seemed like a good place for the stories.

Eddie Tipton, back, and his brother Tommy Tipton appear at the Polk County Courthouse Thursday, June 29, 2017. Eddie Tipton, the cyber security expert and brainpower behind a lottery rigging scandal that netted $2 million in illegal winnings from five state lotteries, pleaded guilty Thursday to a felony charge of ongoing criminal conduct charge. Photo: Rodney White/The Register

The fact that Tommy Tipton was "The Law" in his parts, and was even on a SWAT team, meant he had "all the night toys that you can imagine." We think he meant night-vision goggles and things like that.

"I started hitting the woods," Tommy Tipton said, in search for Bigfoot.

In Louisiana, Tommy Tipton watched "these animals," he told an Iowa state prosecutor later. "Something happened to me in Louisiana where I actually watched these animals for a couple of hours, and I've been hooked ever since. I used to spend all my spare cash, you know, on deer leases. Now, I don't do that anymore."

He had better things to track.

"I go out in the woods and hunt this creature, in which you are humiliated and laughed at by others," presumably over believing in Bigfoot and not due to your use of such poor grammar.

Tommy described his brother Eddie as "a very large man" who lived alone. "And he's kind of lonesome and lonely."

The brothers would talk frequently. Sometimes they talked about travel plans, which is how Tommy came to tell Eddie he was headed to Colorado, Tommy Tipton testified in legal proceedings.

"Then he asked, you know, do I ever play the lottery, and I told him, 'Yes.' He told me, if you want to play, he had some numbers if I was interested in playing."

Tommy Tipton had questions.

"I'm like, 'Where did you get the numbers?'"

Eddie told him he had a legal pad sheet full of numbers. But not just any numbers—like Bigfoot's birthday or inseam.

"He told me that it was an analysis of numbers that were due to come up," Tommy Tipton recalled Eddie saying. Tommy immediately thought of people who tracked numbers, like Stanford-educated statistician Joan Ginther, who won millions from four scratch games sold by stores that sometimes held tickets for her after she figured out patterns that showed a win was coming. The woman lived a "nightmare" of police escorts to the grocery store, and other inconveniences, Tommy Tipton recalled.

Even knowing he might risk a life of inconvenient trips to grocery stores, Tommy Tipton somehow soldiered on with Eddie's yellow-pad numbers in hand. He played them, visiting several stores.

"I did go to Colorado," Tommy Tipton said. The mountains are hard to forget, especially if you're from Texas. "I played those numbers and the ticket won."

He had bought "a bunch" of tickets, with Eddie's numbers and others. Twelve years later, when prosecutors were asking about it, he couldn't remember how many tickets he bought.

Eddie Tipton had told his brother that Eddie couldn't buy the tickets because of his job in the lottery industry. But Tommy could play legally, Eddie assured him.

When Tommy Tipton isn't searching for Bigfoot, he works with other large animals. "I'm a horseman. I'm a horse-shoer. I deal with lots of horses," he said. You know, horses.

This is relevant because Tommy called a lawyer friend of his who was busy trying to buy horses. Except this was a matter wholly unrelated to the equine world. You hate to look a gift lottery win in the mouth, but Tommy wondered if he detected a slight stench around this whole thing.

Tommy wanted to know if he could legally buy lottery tickets using numbers from his lottery-agency-employee-brother who had analyzed numbers that might be hot plays soon.

So he asked a horse-trader, who happened to be a lawyer.

The horseman-lawyer said he'd have to check into it. A couple of days later, he told Tommy, "I cannot find where it's illegal for you to play." Tommy didn't know that Thad Whisenant, the lawyer, had copied the numbers and later was believed to have played the same drawing as Tommy, eventually winning a third of the jackpot under a Las Vegas corporation whose name is Spanish for "Question of Luck."

Tommy Tipton headed to Colorado—and not just for the lottery intrigue. He was on vacation.

"I went to a wildlife management area where there was a gentleman [who] was run out of a wildlife management area by some animal," Tommy Tipton told prosecutors.

Bigfoot?

Tommy had to know. He went to the wildlife area, but he got coffee first. You don't just go out and look for Bigfoot in broad daylight, he explained. "When you do this hobby, it's not something you do really in the middle of the day or the afternoon. You do it once nightfall comes and you do it all night long until morning."

So, heck, an all-night hunt necessitates coffee. "You do drink a lot of coffee," Tipton explained later in legal proceedings.

Tipton was ready to make the connection between Bigfoot, coffee futures, and a major lottery scam. You see, he wasn't just after coffee.

"Whenever I stopped to get coffee or whenever I would stop and get gas, I would buy [lottery] tickets," he said, all over Colorado, in this case. For two and a half days. He filled out a bunch of slips with 30 or 40 of Eddie's well-researched numbers. One set of them scored the $4.8 million Colorado in-state jackpot programmed by Eddie Tipton.

Tommy Tipton, perhaps still worried about the stench of it all, told fellow Bigfoot hunter Alexander Hicks, a friend, about the win and asked him to turn in the ticket to claim the cash. It's like a fraternity, you know, Bigfoot hunters. Not everyone meets the standards to be part of the exclusive club, but Hicks did, in Tipton's view. They had met through an organization of Bigfoot hunters. Hicks had street cred, or maybe dark-field or dimly-lit forest cred.

Tipton mentioned that his brother, Eddie, worked for a lottery association. He also mentioned having marital problems. For those reasons, Tommy Tipton didn't want to personally redeem the ticket. He figured Hicks could.

"I didn't think there would be a problem," Tipton later told prosecutors.

A week or two later, Hicks turned the ticket in. Tipton had offered Hicks a share of the prize for his trouble. The prize after taxes and the shares for the other two winners came to $568,900. Again, two other winners split the overall prize, including Tommy's number-copying lawyer, Whisenant.

Tommy Tipton stashed the cash. Eventually, it was spent.

How? He said he loaned Eddie, his brother, $100,000 to help pay for Eddie's eye-grabbing, large home.

"He was building this monster of a house and I loaned him a hundred [thousand dollars]," Tommy Tipton recalled in testimony.

The agreement was for Eddie to pay the money back when he sold the house. Six months later, Tommy loaned Eddie another $75,000. Eddie claimed he also donated some of it to his church—he thinks $20,000 or $25,000—because he wanted it to amount to a tithe. He gave as much as $40,000, he didn't remember exactly, to a missionary group that was headed to Mexico.

For some reason, Hicks brought all new bills to Tommy Tipton. "Every time I pulled new bills out to purchase something, people would look at you funny," Tipton said. He swapped $100,000 for consecutive bills, but no one seems to know why. Fearing trouble, he tried to trade cash with a local fireworks dealer, who called the FBI because he suspected Tommy was money-laundering.

eleven

TOMMY FALLS OUT OF A TREE HUNTING BIGFOOT; THE FBI COMES CALLING

When the FBI came calling to look into suspected money-laundering, Tommy Tipton was in the hospital. He spent a week or so being treated for injuries he sustained when he fell 31 feet out of a tree while looking for Bigfoot, he testified.

"I almost died," he told prosecutors. "Shattered both my legs."

Authorities couldn't immediately give a condition report on Bigfoot. It was unclear if Tipton saw the Big Fella that day.

Tommy Tipton had no idea the FBI was checking into the lottery win. Agents talked to him again when he got out of the hospital. He recalled that the agents had laughed at him over the Bigfoot hobby. Tipton wasn't laughing. He was in a wheelchair and in a lot of pain. And he takes this stuff seriously, as would anyone willing to risk a 31-foot fall from a tree in the name of a hobby.

The FBI agents asked Tommy Tipton how a fire started in the broom closet of the steakhouse he owned in Texas. Tipton said it wasn't intentionally set, and in fact, he had sold the restaurant, and the sale would be official in a week.

The investigators wanted to know where he got the money for the restaurant. Realizing they already knew, he said he won the Colorado lottery.

In an odd twist, the lawyer who Tipton had consulted before buying tickets, Whisenant, and a La Grange, Texas lawyer named Luis Vallejo, were connected to one of the other winning tickets that split the jackpot with Tommy Tipton in Colorado. The spring after the Colorado jackpot win, Vallejo, who was in regular contact with Whisenant before and after the Colorado win, tried to deposit $250,000 in five LLC accounts at a La Grange, Texas bank without his name associated.

"It was a big shock to me to hear that an attorney whom I went for advice played the lottery," apparently with Eddie's numbers, Tommy told prosecutors later.

A local Texas prosecutor of traffic cases told Tommy, who besides being justice of the peace was a reserve police officer and a former sheriff's deputy in the area, he should resign as an administrative law judge "because of the appearance that I'm not trustworthy now. Talk about a knife in the heart," Tommy recalled. Basically, he was told to resign, and the authorities wouldn't act to remove him from office. The local prosecutor told Tipton he'd need a lawyer. His suggestion? Luis Vallejo.

Vallejo basically said no thanks and good luck. And why not? He already had cash from Colorado.

Robert Shapiro, the Colorado assistant attorney general, later asked Tommy Tipton what advice he wanted from Vallejo when he called him. Tipton said he wanted to know if he could play numbers presented by someone else, someone with some connection to the lottery. Vallejo basically said no. "Should that have been the end of your analysis?" Shapiro asked Tommy Tipton during an interview with prosecutors.

"For Vallejo it would have been," Tommy said. "It wasn't for me, I guess, because I'm not him."

Tommy Tipton had played the numbers Eddie gave him, but he also played birth dates of his children and wedding anniversary dates, just for good measure.

His winning ticket was from the list of numbers that his brother, the future felon, had given him.

But two others had winning tickets as well, and one, the Cuestion de Suerte, or "Question of Luck" claim, also used Eddie Tipton's numbers.

Hicks and Whisenant also claimed winning tickets.

Tommy Tipton noticed when Vallejo bought a building or two next to the courthouse in La Grange after that lotto win.

Iowa Division of Criminal Investigation agent Don Smith asked if Eddie Tipton had told Tommy that the numbers would win. No, he didn't, Tommy replied. "He did not say they were winners. He told me these are numbers that are due to come up. He didn't say I was gonna win. He never, ever said I was gonna win."

Tommy didn't even play all the numbers, with millions of dollars on the line. He said filling out the slips became monotonous. He got tired. He went to several stores because he feared that the clerk who had to feed the numbers into the machine would consider it "a pain in the rear," he later told prosecutors.

twelve
ON (TO) WISCONSIN

Eddie's friend, Robert Rhodes, visited Tipton in Iowa. He was in a bad mood. He was recently divorced and living with his mother. Eddie thought he could help. He went way back with Rhodes, who was CEO of Systems Evolution Inc. from 1996-2003 while Tipton was chief operating officer there.

"Hey, I might have this opportunity if you're interested," Eddie said in 2007

Tipton told Rhodes he would write down some numbers he could play, the money would be his if he won, and Tipton would stay out of it—other than providing numbers that couldn't lose because he had rigged the system. He told him what day to buy the ticket or tickets, knowing that the computers knew the three magic dates when the stars would align like some rare celestial event, if those were set by the heavens.

As was the case in Colorado, it didn't even matter what game Rhodes played. Tipton had it set up so the numbers would work on any of the local games. The mother of all multi-state lottery games, the national Powerball, wasn't involved in the scheme because those numbers were drawn using balls, not one of Eddie's programmed computers.

Rhodes was skeptical. He doubted everything was a sure-fire jackpot as Tipton suggested.

Rhodes would later testify that he rented a car in Des Moines and drove to Wisconsin with a stack of 3 X 5 index cards loaded with the number combinations from Tipton. He had instructions to play them all, to make sure he played combinations for several straight drawings, and to ensure that he was in the game on December 29, 2007.

Rhodes bought the tickets, choosing the numbers to be entered in the lottery terminal for a Wisconsin Megabuck in-state jackpot that would be decided by a MUSL random-number generator. He drove back to Des Moines, then flew back home to Texas. It was there that he checked the numbers online and realized Eddie's numbers had won the jackpot on December 29.

The jackpot was $2 million if the winner chose an annuity, or $783,257 if the winner took the lump-sum option. As if to foreshadow the Iowa scandal, Rhodes tried to claim the win without giving his name. No dice, the Wisconsin gambling powers said. He said he'd create a trust. Officials said fine, if he named who was in charge. Rhodes sued to get the money. In the end, he won a court order to receive payment through a corporation called Delta S. Holdings.

This time, Tipton got $40,000 of the $783,257 in four $10,000 bundles—for his trouble.

Remarkably, Tipton asked Rhodes to bilk Wisconsin again in 2010. Rhodes testified that he wasn't crazy about the idea, but he flew to Chicago, drove to Wisconsin, and nervously bought tickets for another December 29 draw, this time in 2010. Because he was nervous, Rhodes decided not to play all the numbers Tipton gave him, even though this time it was only a few notecards.

After Rhodes returned to Texas, the drawing occurred and he checked the numbers online. The winning numbers were among those that Rhodes had not played.

But he wasn't done with Tipton and his jackpots. Months later, Tipton would pull another winning ticket—this one for a $16.5 million jackpot—from inside a paperback book, and ask Rhodes to cash it.

thirteen
IOWA, THE TALL PRIZE STATE

Someone hit it big in Des Moines in December 2010, scoring a $16.5 million jackpot on a ticket purchased at that north Des Moines convenience store, part of the QuikTrip chain.

Almost a month later, no one had claimed the prize. So as part of the lottery's usual due diligence, Rich and Neubauer faced the TV cameras again for an announcement on January 28, 2011.

"It's nearly been a month since we announced we had a $16.5 million Hot Lotto winner," Rich said. Behind him were colorful Iowa Lottery posters and an oversized check written out to "Is It You?" The memo line on the fake check read, "Double-Check Your Tickets!"

Rich wore a tasteful blue blazer and blue dress shirt with a red tie. His reading glasses dangled from his lapel pocket. A Radio Iowa microphone stood in front of him.

"The Iowa Lottery has been looking and asking everyone to please check their tickets," Rich said. Somehow, every time he appeared at one of these news conferences, you could almost imagine him saying, "Ladies and gentlemen, welcome to Ringling Brothers and Barnum & Bailey Circus." He projects well. He always seems enthusiastic.

"As CEO, I wanted to announce that I believe that the person who has purchased or owns this ticket probably doesn't know that they have it," Rich told the news conference. A slide appeared that read, "The jackpot-winning ticket was purchased at QuikTrip, 4801 N.E. 14th St. in Des Moines." It is a convenience store in an industrial/commercial area near Interstate Highway 80.

Rich isn't wrong all that much. Here, he was. The person who bought the ticket knew full well he had the winner. He had made sure of that.

For reasons that aren't fully understood, but are certainly appreciated, the sound under the video of the news conference, at least on the YouTube recording, features the hot Latin vibe of a trumpet.

Tom Gehrke, who was division manager at QuikTrip, joined Rich on camera and said maybe this was a drive-by ticket buy for a visitor traveling down I-80. If the visitor was driving down I-80, the locals hope they were driving very quickly and were good at dodging trucks. The store isn't far from the interchange of Interstates 35 and 80, a well-known crossroads for the nation's truck drivers. We would call them over-the-road truckers but we've never understood who drives under the road.

"We thought it might be someone who was just passing through because it's an interstate store. We just don't know," Gehrke said.

Wrong again.

"We're just waiting to see it," Gehrke added. "Obviously, there is a lot of buzz."

Rich then noted winners often take some time to contact accountants and lawyers to help with a life-changing experience. He noted that this ticket had numbers for drawings on different days, so perhaps the person was waiting for all the drawings to pass.

A slide displayed the winning numbers for the drawing on December 29, 2010: 3, 12, 16, 26, 33 and a Hot Ball of 11.

"Someone has the ticket. The Iowa Lottery wants to give away the money," Rich said. "We want someone to come in so we can show you the money, give you the money." Perhaps he was channeling his best 1996's "Jerry Maguire": "Show me the money!"

"Somewhere out there is a heck of a ticket worth $16.5 million," said Rich.

It was a heck of a ticket, all right.

In January or February 2011, Tipton visited Rhodes in Houston. Rhodes apologized for blowing the jackpot play in December 2010 by failing to use all the numbers.

Terry Rich at the Iowa Lottery Press Conference on December 29, 2011 announcing the winning Hot Lotto jackpot ticket has been found. Source: Iowa Lottery

Tipton then pulled out a paperback book and pulled from the pages the Hot Lotto ticket he bought in northern Des Moines. Tipton explained that this was the winning ticket from the December 29, 2010, 17-state Hot Lotto drawing in Iowa. The ticket was the sole winner of the $16.5 million jackpot. Tipton said he wanted his brother Tommy to redeem the ticket, but Eddie was concerned about raising suspicions among FBI agents because Tommy had won a 2005 prize that drew questions. So Tipton gave Rhodes the ticket and said Rhodes could claim it.

Nearly a year later, the winning ticket arrived at Iowa Lottery headquarters in Des Moines. It was December 29, 2011.

"Ladies and gentlemen, we have the winning ticket," Rich told the media, holding the ticket up in his right hand. "But we don't know the person nor all of the background about this winning ticket."

He introduced Beau Gamble and Julie Johnson McLean of the large and widely respected Davis Brown law firm in Des Moines.

McLean said the firm represented the person who won the prize. The lawyers submitted the claim form. "Now the Iowa Lottery will do its standard investigative protocols. And now I will turn it over to Terry Rich," she said. And that was it.

McLean didn't identify the prizewinner, or even mention that the person wanted to remain anonymous. Beau didn't say a word. But both lawyers smiled a lot. And McLean noted that they were "excited."

And why wouldn't they be? The Davis Brown firm was promised $500,000 for its trouble but later negotiated $50,000 in lawyer fees and a $1 million "contingent fee" if the prize was claimed. It wasn't, and the firm was left waiting years for the $50,000.

Another thing that didn't come up: Davis Brown represented the Iowa Lottery in matters of intellectual property and trademark—and still does. The Lottery's general counsel at the time had to waive a potential conflict of interest to allow Davis Brown to represent Shaw and Hexham, noted Rob Porter, vice president and general counsel for the lottery since 2014.

At the news conference, Rich noted that the lawyers had submitted the winning ticket with an hour and 50 minutes to spare. Ding! Ding! Ding! Something stunk.

"We still are learning details as part of our security protocols and procedures," Rich said, holding the ticket up in full camera view, a bit higher than his shoulder. He later said he wished he hadn't done that because it revealed security codes and numbers on the ticket. It basically enabled bogus claims to the prize to sound more convincing, though no more valid or successful.

"Of course, security and integrity are at the heart of what the Iowa Lottery is all about," Rich said at the news conference. In fact, in July 2011, the Iowa Lottery spent $100,000 on new random-number generators and related equipment. Eddie Tipton wrote the codes for them.

Rich noted the ticket was signed by Hexham Investments Trust, Crawford Shaw of Bedford, N.Y., trustee.

Lottery officials normally would pay the prize at this point, but "this is an unusual circumstance," Rich said. Things needed to be checked, including the prize amount. That's because the lotteries offer an annuity option that had changed with interest rates. The ticket was worth $10.75 million cash. But falling interest rates had dropped the annuity value to $14.29 million, from the original $16.5 million.

Rich said he didn't know how long the investigation would take.

"Of course, we're thrilled the ticket came in and has been presented before the deadline. This will assure those folks who might be out there looking through their underwear drawers or the top of their [vehicle] visors or some other location that we have the ticket that we know was purchased one year ago today."

Then he said he wanted to make sure the right person was paid, because thousands buy tickets on a regular basis.

Rich noted that a trust could be used to claim the prize, but the lottery would need the name of the person who bought the ticket.

Bogle told reporters that lottery officials would track the ticket from its purchase to the presentation of the ticket at the lottery. He noted that the ticket was, in fact, the one bought at the Des Moines convenience store.

A reporter asked if the person in the security-camera footage from the store had to be the one who presented the ticket. "Not necessarily," Rich explained. "You can gift a ticket. You can gift a ticket to a minor, even though they can't buy a ticket."

"We have to make sure we can follow the trail."

Rich's next comment was full of intrigue, as things turned out, but at the time it probably seemed as innocent as he meant it to be.

"We have no reason to believe that this has any implications of any impropriety," Rich said. "We just got the ticket."

A reporter asked if the convenience store security video would be used in the investigation. "Yes," Bogle responded.

That was an understatement. Pored over, analyzed, heavily scrutinized. "Used" was probably too weak a word, because the Lottery had been subjected to an almost unimaginable string of people claiming they were the winner.

Dave Jobes, assistant director of the Iowa Division of Criminal Investigation, started working the case in 2013 when he took his job. He recalled the many would-be winners who called the DCI directly, rather than join the group of questionable claimants who contacted Iowa Lottery headquarters.

"After we released the video of the ticket purchase, that snippet of video from the convenience store when the ticket was bought, we started getting calls, emails and other inquiries from individuals who were convinced—or at least were trying to convince us—that they had purchased the ticket and they had lost it, or it had been taken from them or they simply misplaced it and couldn't remember what happened to it," Jobes recalled. "But they were certain it was them and they were the true winner," Jobes added with a smile.

How did DCI weed through the cascade of "winners"?

"Each of those claims were vetted, some more easily than others," Jobes said. "Some we could get through pretty quickly by looking into their story. We could show that they weren't in the area at the time that the ticket was purchased, or they didn't know what store it was purchased from, or some other key element told us that they certainly were not the original ticket purchaser."

In response to a reporter's question about the mood at the lottery headquarters when the ticket was presented, Rich said it replaced a year of "my dog ate it, or I lost it in the wash" with an "adrenaline rush."

"This is exciting for employees," who like to give prize money to legitimate winners, Rich noted.

A couple of weeks later, Shaw, the New York lawyer and trustee who had signed the ticket on behalf of the Belizean trust Hexham Investment, traveled to Iowa to discuss the ticket on behalf of his client—Eddie Tipton, who was still anonymous.

Thomas H. Miller, Iowa's deputy attorney general at the time, found Shaw uncooperative. Eventually the Iowa prosecutors threatened to file felony charges—albeit for what Miller considered a "low-level felony"—against Shaw, and he agreed to talk to Miller on the phone. It was snowing that day in Iowa, and Miller missed his office Christmas party to grill Shaw for a bit.

"I recall him being very resistant to disclosing much information," said Miller. "He didn't even admit that [Houston lawyer Robert L.] Sonfield and Rhodes were the parties who had hired him. However, he stipulated that he wouldn't deny that those were the parties that had hired him. More interesting to me was that his expected fee on this transaction was as much as a half-million dollars, which is quite a bit of money for someone to do the ministerial act of cashing in a ticket."

Shaw didn't identify the person who bought the ticket, and the Iowa Lottery didn't pay.

By the end of the month, facing a deadline, Shaw withdrew the claim, apparently without asking anyone else involved, Rich said in an interview later.

After the case concluded, Bogle said, "The only reason you withdraw a ticket is to keep your rear end out of jail. I remember thinking this truly was a fraud. We didn't know how they did it yet. It wasn't over."

By August 8, 2012, Rich was giving the lottery a 50-50 chance of solving the case. Ten days later, he said authorities would consider releasing the video of the ticket being purchased at the Des Moines convenience store. A year later, the case was still unsolved. Six months after that, lottery officials were in touch with Canadian authorities, looking into lawyer Philip Johnston, who had asked Shaw to present the ticket.

In early October, there was news of a limited immunity deal, presumably for Johnston.

That led to Houston, home of Tommy Tipton and associates.

In October 2014, news accounts noted that the hunt for the mystery winner was still on. Rich stood before the cameras, again.

But by the time January 15, 2015 rolled around, an arrest had been made.

"MUSL employee arrested in Hot Lotto jackpot mystery," read the headline on the Lottery Post website. Eddie Raymond Tipton, who was 51 at the time, had been charged with trying to cash the Hot Lotto ticket.

Once again, after extensive preparation, Iowa Lottery's team faced the cameras with a major announcement. Minutes before the news conference started, the staff handed out a news release.

"You've got to be shitting me!" exclaimed one camera operator, expressing some degree of surprise at the turn of events.

Jobes told an audience at a news conference in January 2015 that tips had flooded in after the release of the snippet of security-camera video. "The Iowa Division of Criminal investigation, along with the Iowa attorney general's office, have filed charges and made an arrest in the Hot Lotto investigation this afternoon. Eddie Raymond Tipton, age 51, of Norwalk, Iowa, has been arrested and charged with two counts of fraud, both felonies," Jobes said as he stood in front of an American flag. "Mr. Tipton was arrested without incident and taken into custody at approximately 2:16 this afternoon."

Jobes noted that Tipton worked for MUSL and was banned from buying lottery tickets, but had done just that at the Des Moines store. He noted that Tipton tried to claim the ticket with the help of others. "This is an active and ongoing investigation," Jobes noted.

Rich then told the reporters assembled that he was "disappointed" someone in the industry—a vendor for the Iowa Lottery—had tried to bilk Iowa out of $16 million. "At the same time, we're gratified that the thorough procedures and protocols we've developed to protect the security and integrity of our games worked to prevent the payment of a disputed prize. This truly is one of the strangest situations in the history of lotteries. We believe this is the largest lottery jackpot ever to be claimed, only to have that claim withdrawn."

The case focused on "possible fraud attempts" in the claiming of the prize, Rich noted. "It was the right thing for our lottery to refuse to pay this jackpot prize unless and until basic security questions about it could be answered, and they never were.

"We all know there always will be people who will try to beat the system," he said, and the lottery planned to update procedures to prevent that.

A reporter asked what turned out to be a huge question, but Rich moved through it quickly. "He didn't manipulate the game in any way, did he? He just bought the ticket that happened to win?" the reporter queried.

Rich responded: "Good question. This charge is based solely on his purchase and attempt to cash a winning ticket. There are no allegations of anything else. Obviously, the investigation continues." Jobes stood stone-faced over Rich's right shoulder, next to the flag.

Jobes then confirmed that the charges stemmed from the fact that Tipton was not allowed to play, because he worked for MUSL, of which Iowa Lottery is a member.

Someone asked if there would be more arrests outside of Iowa.

Jobes responded: "It's an ongoing investigation."

Someone asked what changes were being made to security. Bogle took that one. "We have made changes, and we are constantly looking for vulnerabilities…and we put in processes, procedures, and technologies to mitigate those. Obviously, I can't speak specifically about those because the more people know about the more they would try to figure out how to get around." He noted some procedures had been changed after the Hot Lotto case involving Tipton.

And the money? It was split among the states. Iowa's share went into a special promotion, "Mystery Millionaire," which was won, perhaps poetically, by a retired police officer, Dean Stuhr, Rich said. Stuhr's prize: $1 million. Legit. Others won $25,000, $50,000, or $100,000 in a series of on-stage drawings at the Iowa State Fair. "It's just overwhelming," Stuhr told Neubauer on stage.

Iowa Lottery officials had worked side-by-side with law enforcement, which reinforced the fact, and optics, that the Lottery was involved in the investigation, not the target of it. MUSL, on the other hand, went to "no comment" and immediately fired Tipton.

A couple of months later, Robert Rhodes of Sugar Land, Texas was arrested on charges of fraud.

The case turned into a crucial point in lottery history as investigators first established circumstantial evidence that Eddie Tipton had committed a fraud, and then cracked the code, showing how he had told the computer how to cheat, and when. It was an appalling breach of trust and a clear fraud, an unexpected crack in the façade of an industry that had been known for tight security, cameras, elaborate office check-in procedures, surveillance cameras and background checks.

Three months later after Rhodes was arrested came this: "BOMBSHELL: MUSL employee might have rigged Hot Lotto computerized drawing" trumpeted the Lottery Post, which led its story with the fact that it had been warning of potential computer drawing frauds at lotteries.

Iowa state prosecutors laid out a case of circumstantial evidence they said showed Eddie Tipton tampered with computers used to draw winning numbers and the monitoring camera in the computer room at MUSL headquarters. The camera took images once a minute instead of every second as it should have per MUSL protocol.

Tipton had programmed the computers to use his code to limit the universe only if the drawing were on a Wednesday or a Saturday, after 8 p.m. Central Standard Time, and on one of three calendar dates (assuming it wasn't a leap year): May 27, November 23, December 29. Those happened to be dates Tipton often left town for holidays.

Even the part of the random program that was tied to a radioactive isotope couldn't stop Tipton from altering a system that he, of course, designed.

"Any change in protocol or process by the Multi-State Lottery may have thrown his scheme off completely. It was truly only the ability to have both access to the machine and enough knowledge about how security protocols and draw processes worked that allowed him to anticipate what the numbers could be," Rich said.

Tipton had the code on his work computer, which he used to run thousands of test draws to come up with likely picks, which he played himself or fed to his allies, Porter said.

In late July 2015, Tipton was found guilty on charges related only to the Iowa drawing, and was sentenced to 10 years.

After the verdict, juror Dennis Buswell told Des Moines TV station KCCI he thought Tipton was clearly guilty. The jury had found Tipton guilty after about six hours of deliberation. "Everything about the case, even though there wasn't a lot of hard evidence, led back to the defendant," Buswell said. "Whether it was phone calls, the people he associated with, the people he worked with…"

Another juror, Laura Vangundy, told KCCI the jury was sure that Tipton committed the crime: "He had the knowledge. We looked at the tape from the QuikTrip over and over [for an hour], and we were able to tell that the man did look like [Eddie Tipton]. We watched him as he went out of the store. It was the same [vehicle] that was rented."

Neubauer recalled many in the public most likely thought that was the end of the case.

Jobes and his investigators weren't so sure.

"As investigators, we had some pretty strong suspicions that was not the end of the story. The agents working it really had a sense that, 'That can't be it. There has to be more out there.' I give those agents a lot of credit for continuing to dig and to pursue all those other leads, even after that conviction," Jobes said. "That's what I'm really proud of, that the agents who were working it knew there was more to the story, and they weren't going to let it go."

"After the initial conviction of Eddie Tipton, from a public perspective that seemed like a stopping point, maybe," Jobes said. "Of course, the agents didn't stop there; they had the good sense that there was more to the story. They had evidence suggesting there was more to the story, and they continued to pursue it.

"I can remember getting inquiries from reporters from different media outlets saying, 'What's the big deal? Why are you still chasing the story? Isn't this a waste of time?'"

fourteen
PUBLIC TRUST, VIOLATED

"You have to put this into perspective of public trust, and the nature of what was done," Jobes said. "We had an employee in an organization who abused his position for personal gain, is kind of what it comes down to. That had the potential to erode trust in not just the Iowa Lottery but lotteries across the country because that employee was tied to MUSL and all these multi-state games."

The $80 billion gamble: Could Iowa's persistence cost the entire nation its lottery business, much like Louisiana did in the 1800s?

"While the ticket was not paid in Iowa because of security procedures Iowa Lottery had in place, it pointed to this larger case of fraud. It was important to chase that to the end," Jobes said.

"As investigators, we don't want to stop at a convenient point with an initial good result. We want to make sure that we have vetted every angle in the case, sought out every act of wrongdoing we can find, and made sure that's presented to the courts or the prosecutors to be handled accordingly. That's what the agents did in this case," Jobes added.

Two Iowa agents, Matt Anderson and Don Smith, kept the case moving. "Don Smith, in particular at the end—he's a bulldog," Jobes said. "He got ahold of this case and he chased every lead he could find to the bitter end."

No doubt, the two lead agents had help from their colleagues, Jobes said. "[Smith and Anderson] are modest enough agents that they won't take credit for the work that they did, but I'm more than happy to give them credit. They were the ones calling the shots from an investigative standpoint and really did a great job chasing this thing down."

The Iowa cyber-crimes unit—which mostly chases child pornography predatory sex crimes cases and is backlogged for months—was involved in the case due to the computer analysis. The state brought in help from other states in this case as well.

Tipton appealed the initial conviction.

The case grew over time into a broader, multistate scandal. Tipton continued to maintain his innocence.

fifteen

WHAT HAPPENED, STRAIGHT FROM EDDIE'S MOUTH

Those were the basics, but the details—culled in part from Eddie's own words—are compelling.

Tipton spent $25 on lotto tickets on December 23 at the north Des Moines convenience store for the drawing on December 29, 2010. It was one of maybe a dozen or more stops he made to buy tickets.

Tipton peeled off a $50 bill at the Des Moines store. He had two play slips in his pocket, already made out. He had chosen his own numbers rather than let the computer pick them.

He could have rigged the whole thing, down to a certain set of numbers—instead of dozens of possible combinations—except for a check-and-balance system that proved fatal to Tipton's scheme.

"He could have rigged everything, but that would have made the fraud far easier to spot," Porter said in an interview. "If the same numbers show up over and over, or show up repeatedly on the same dates, that would have been suspect. That was a clever touch in the Tipton scheme."

Eddie's numbers were special.

He claims he didn't think the ticket would win, which is why he felt comfortable buying it himself—with his face obscured by a hat and a hoodie and a general air of not wanting to be seen from behind, where the camera was.

"I didn't think it was gonna work because of the way...The [Random-Number Generator, or RNG computer] had been around a long time," Tipton told Sand.

He knew the machine would be scheduled to be replaced. "And so I figured, hey...I'll give it a try. But if they had changed any of the settings then it would have made it moot." Useless.

The computer could have been set to run any number of tests to prove it was randomly drawing numbers, but if it was still running 500 pre-draws, and the same order of game draws, Tipton's fraud would work. The number of tests and actual drawings involved was important.

Tipton claimed he didn't know any ticket he bought would be invalid under MUSL rules. He said he knew the policy was that he couldn't play, but he didn't know he was legally banned from doing so. In fact, he added, perhaps somewhat cavalierly, "There were states that actually encouraged me to play their games because they wanted the revenue." Colorado wouldn't give him a ticket, but New Mexico and New Hampshire said: "Yeah. Play. We could use the money," he said.

Tipton won $5 on a New Mexico ticket and left it sitting unclaimed in his house.

In Iowa, Tipton recalled visiting several Des Moines area convenience stores, among other locations. Afterward, Tipton held a ticket with the winning $16.5 million jackpot combination, and one other set of numbers was good for a 3 + 1 win that was far smaller.

"I'm no mathematician, but the odds of having both a 3 + 1 and a jackpot winner on the same ticket always seem unusually long," Porter recalled. "That was the first indication to me that fraud was involved, before we knew anything further about Tipton and how he committed the scheme."

And here's another interesting tidbit investigators turned up later: Tipton and Rhodes exchanged seven phone calls the day that the $16.5 million Hot Lotto prize was won.

Tipton drove to Texas and gave the ticket, tucked into a book, to his pal Rhodes in Houston before leaving to return to Iowa after his Christmas vacation. He told Rhodes to keep the ticket until it could be redeemed later when the hubbub of someone winning died down. He also gave Rhodes the hooded jacket he had worn into the convenience store in Des Moines, which seems like a guilty man covering his tracks.

"I wasn't wearing it anymore," Tipton said of the jacket, which had been immortalized by a security camera. "I knew the video was out, so there was no reason to wear it." He didn't want it around anymore.

"You know, do a claim a little bit later in case the excitement had died down," Tipton told Sand. "And then later I remember having a discussion, you know, about whether we should claim it at all. And I was thinking, well, you know, it's big."

Everything was big about this case. Tipton was big. The whole situation was a big gamble. The potential for trouble was big.

"You know, it was unexpected to be this big, and so we should, you know, consider not doing it," Tipton recalled thinking.

Rhodes and Tipton were sitting in a restaurant when they checked the numbers online and confirmed the ticket had won.

When Rhodes started to balk at cashing the ticket, Tipton said he could bring in his brother to do the dirty work. But Rhodes seemed to have his own needs. He had just been hit with a big SEC fraud fine that was detailed later by the Daily Beast.

"Well, I can use my brother. But you know, I don't know if that's a good thing to do. It's a big ticket," Tipton told his buddy and future partner in fraud.

The ticket sat for a while until Tipton told Rhodes: "Yeah, go ahead and make a claim if you think you can do it, and make sure your name is not on it and definitely not my name. I don't want anything...everything tied back to me at all."

Tipton knew the state had video of him buying the ticket.

He heard that from Rich. The Iowa Lottery chief had been at a MUSL meeting with then-MUSL Executive Director Chuck Strutt and ran into Tipton, who asked if anyone had claimed the big prize.

"Terry is kind of a media hog," Tipton told Sand. "And so there were cameras there at one point in time so he kept coming by and checking on stuff. And then one time while he was there he was talking about this

Hot Lotto ticket and that they had seen the video, and that, you know, he said he thinks he's from the military, he said "yes sir" you know. But we can't make him out.

"And so I knew there was a video at that time."

Rich recalled in an interview that, as a board member, he visited MUSL from time to time. Rich had heard that the lottery's investigators thought the lottery winner was from southern Iowa (probably imported from Missouri) because the video hinted at a southern drawl, and the person kept saying, "Yes sir," like any polite Southerner would, we suppose.

"I was at MUSL [in 2011] and I was talking to Chuck Strutt, the executive director (at the time) and Eddie walked up," Rich recalled. "They were asking about it and I said, 'Yeah, we have the video and we have someone with a southern drawl. I didn't notice Eddie's reaction, but at that point he knew we had video."

Bogle said he didn't want to release the video to the public until leads were pursued. "There were pros and cons to that. Obviously, some in the public thought the case might have been solved sooner if we had, but I didn't want to pull up to Lottery headquarters on a Monday morning and see 50 big stocky guys dressed in a black hoodie and a black coat waiting in line: 'I'm the guy who bought the ticket!' I didn't want to deal with that.

"It was like the video, to keep with the gambling theme, was our ace up our sleeve because we hadn't released it so we would know if someone was lying or not, or taking us down a rabbit hole somewhere," Bogle said.

After exhausting the leads, Lottery officials decided to release the video.

After the video was released in October 2014, Rich was at MUSL again when he encountered Tipton.

"I was out in the MUSL parking lot talking to Chuck Strutt at the same time Eddie Tipton walked out. As we looked at the video initially and someone said it's Eddie Tipton, Steve Bogle discounted that it could be because [the person in the video] wasn't big enough. The perspective of the camera wasn't big enough. So, we were looking at other leads for a few days.

"Eddie just happened to be standing there, so I said, 'Hey, Eddie, where did you grow up? He said, 'Houston, Texas.' I said, 'Did you ever know a guy named Robert Rhodes?' I was one of the few who knew Rhodes' name and because the investigators felt strongly at the time that it was not Eddie, I thought I'd give it a shot," Rich said. "He said, 'Yeah, he's my best friend.' That was the second 'Ding! Ding! Ding!' for me."

Rich went back to advise Bogle, a good and strategic investigator who went ballistic that Rich had said anything.

"Hey, stay out of the investigation!" Bogle chided his boss.

Rich ultimately thought his questioning of Tipton helped the case, but he realized that his role needed to be to keep the story alive in the media to keep fleshing out the facts of the case.

Porter joined the lottery a month and half before the video of Tipton buying the ticket was released, before anyone had identified Tipton. But he knew about the case, and he thought denying the claim was the right thing to do.

Still, things got interesting quickly.

"I remember Terry Rich coming into my office and shutting the door, which was unusual, and he looked at me and he said, 'We're getting tips. People think the person in the video who bought the Hot Lotto ticket is Eddie Tipton.

"As green as I was, my first reaction was, 'Who is Eddie Tipton?' I had no idea who he was talking about," Porter said. "So, he explained who Eddie Tipton was and his role at the Multi-State Lottery. I am not going to repeat what I said after that. It wasn't in any way appropriate."

Perhaps only four letters per word were needed in this situation.

The heat was on to move quickly on a case "that had been lingering for years," Porter recalled. The statute of limitations was looming. The lottery wanted to give law enforcement all it needed to make the case.

Porter knew he needed to find out everything he could about Tipton. As part of a far broader and more comprehensive effort, he did what many of us might: he Googled Tipton and checked his social media accounts. "It proved to be interesting very quickly," Porter recalled in a video interview for Iowa Lottery archives.

Porter, who became the Iowa Lottery attorney in August 2014, checked out social media and was shocked that an I.T. guy like Eddie

WHAT WAS IN THE MALICIOUS CODE?

Eddie Tipton compiled a malicious computer program (dll) to trigger only if:

- The drawing involved occurred on three specific dates (in November, December or May) when Eddie usually traveled to Texas on vacation.
- The drawing occurred on a Wednesday or Saturday.
- The drawing occurred after 8 p.m.
- The drawing was conducted on one of the two Tipton-programmed RNGs.
- The knowledge of the draw procedures was key

Then: As a result of the malicious code being run, only a small number of combinations could be involved, allowing Tipton to predict the outcome.

Source: Iowa Lottery

---

would leave his accounts public. "Did you know Eddie's social media is wide open?" he asked Rich. That allowed investigators to tie Eddie Tipton to Robert Rhodes, whose social media was also open. The two had worked together at Systems Evolutions Inc., six years before Eddie took the job at MUSL.

"Robert Rhodes had given Eddie Tipton a glowing review on LinkedIn. And the two had gone to the University of Houston together," Porter noted.

Porter knew Rhodes' name was in the mix among investigators' work. "Rhodes and Sonfield for law enforcement were where the road truly ended. They couldn't figure out how the ticket in question got to Rhodes and Sonfield and who had purchased it. So having the link between Eddie Tipton, who had been identified as the purchaser on the video, to Robert Rhodes, the person investigators had known about for a year or more, was significant. It was significant enough for the prosecutors to go to the judge and get search warrants to access Eddie Tipton's phone records and to further develop those leads," Porter said.

But still, investigators had their work cut out for them.

"It was an extremely difficult prosecution for a couple of reasons," Porter recalled. "First of all, the machine used in the December 29, 2010 drawing didn't exist anymore. It was taken out of service by the Multi-State lottery and was wiped. I believe Eddie Tipton had a role in that to help conceal the malicious code that was on the machine. We didn't have enough strong ties or anything other than circumstantial evidence from the ticket going from Eddie Tipton to Robert Rhodes to Johnston and Sonfield. We had some cooperation from Johnston and Sonfield, none from Robert Rhodes at that point. And Mr. Tipton couldn't be forced to testify. So you had to prove a fraud claim with few or no witnesses and no forensic evidence."

They faced a three-year statute of limitations.

Lawyers tell the authors that's a tough place to be.

"It's a huge challenge," but one that Rob Sand—the dogged, if initially reluctant, heir to Thomas H. Miller's case—handled extremely well, Porter said. Well after the case, in the November 2018 general election, Sand ousted incumbent State Auditor Mary Mosiman, so he can look for trouble in a whole range of municipalities and government organizations.

Sand was a few years out of law school. Some wondered if he was up to the job, Porter recalled. "I think he has since proved he was more than up to the task."

Porter had known Sand for a couple of years. They had been involved in a case involving a shady filmmaker looking for film credits in a fraudulent way, and Sand nailed the filmmaker.

In the Tipton case, prosecutors called it an "ongoing crime." The lottery helped investigators with data on prizes and other information on various dates.

Even as the first Tipton trial went on, Oklahoma authorities were asking Iowa investigators to look into Billy and Kyle Conn's case in Oklahoma.

At the same time, Tommy Tipton's testimony from the first trial—with the hot dog comment—caught the attention of an FBI agent who had previously investigated Tommy Tipton for money-laundering. The FBI wondered why a justice of the peace had huge sums of money coming in, unaccounted for. Tommy told agents he won a Colorado state prize many years earlier, and didn't want people, especially his wife, to know about it.

Plus, Robert Rhodes had apparently claimed a state prize in Wisconsin, about the same time all these dots were connected.

"The confluence of those events led us to believe that this was not just an Iowa issue. This had the potential to be a national issue," Porter said.

sixteen
THE INVESTIGATION CONTINUES

At one point, MUSL would ask Tipton to stand where the ticket was purchased to see if he looked the same as the figure in that video from behind, which was the camera angle. Tipton declined.

The fact that this whole saga pitted Tipton against the popular and professional Rich is significant. A proud native of Cooper, Iowa, Rich had done such a good job hyping the centennial celebration for the town—which had 50 residents then and maybe 30 now—that Johnny Carson flew Rich and two other Cooperites to Burbank to appear on the "Tonight Show." Carson was later declared the 51st resident of Cooper. Carson was born in Corning, Iowa, but grew up in neighboring Nebraska.

Rich would go on to make his fortune in cable television and other pursuits and became one of Iowa's most visible and gifted promoters. When Des Moines' zoo was close to broke, Rich came in to run the facility, the Blank Park Zoo, which now has been overhauled, expanded, and is a huge draw for the city.

When Rich took over the Iowa Lottery, he did so with so much enthusiasm that his colleagues sometimes shook their heads, Porter said. "Can we give away a live animal?" Rich once asked.

Rich had prided himself on the layers upon layers of security, the professionalism, the success, and the cash flow to state government that had come with the regular lottery. He was often in front of the cameras, with Mary Neubauer's smooth words, methodically detailing major developments, clarifying any confusion over games or lottery actions, and being transparent.

Transparency was important, because a 2009 report by the Iowa state ombudsman revealed shortcomings in security protocols regarding potential fraud by retailers who sold lottery tickets—criticism that had rung in the ears of lottery staffers for years after. Rich took over the operation that same year and publicly addressed each allegation. Ticket sales at the Iowa Lottery hit record highs, despite the Tipton scandal.

But Rich was not one to stand by and do nothing when it smelled like someone had tampered with a security system seen nearly as impenetrable as a nuclear plant's.

In an interview, Rich recalled that a key moment in the case came in 2010. "We didn't know what was going on. But a unique night that was one of key factors in trying to crack this case came when Eddie Tipton decided to go in and change the time on the computer. He had compiled the code, and the code had four or five variables, and it all had to collide and come together at the same time to make that code go out and say, 'Ok, help me predict and find out what's going on.'"

A colleague wrote down in a log that Tipton had come in to change the clock on the computer from Eastern Daylight Time to standard time. Iowa is in the Central Time Zone.

"That little note, a few years later, was one of the main triggers that told us, 'Well, wait a minute, he went in on that November date— Daylight Saving Time ended three weeks earlier,'" Rich said.

Tipton had written the code to work on one day of the year when the stars aligned like some dark celestial conjunction...with his help.

"Well, lo and behold, December 29, 2010, about 10 minutes after the draw was held, I get an email from staff saying we had a jackpot winner. It was $16.5 million," Rich said.

The numbers had been chosen by the ticket purchaser—not picked by the computer. Everything initially looked fine on the security end, but no one called to claim the prize.

seventeen
ROCK, CHALK, JACKPOT

Tipton also decided to buy a ticket in Kansas, the afternoon after he had bought the Hot Lotto tickets in Des Moines in 2010. He figured it was a buck. No big deal.

Earlier that same day, he had bought Hot Lotto tickets in Iowa and told his co-workers he was heading for vacation in Texas. He played the same numbers on a couple of different plays. He later told Sand that his now-familiar yellow sheets must have fallen into disarray and he used a set twice.

As we now know, Tipton stopped at the convenience store on the north edge of the Des Moines metro, just south of Interstate Highway 80. He ended up buying a ticket that held the jackpot numbers for that upcoming Hot Lotto drawing.

Tipton then headed south, all the way across the metro, then out of state. He later stopped at Kansas City, Kansas and Emporia, Kansas to buy gas and get a drink and some Kansas 2X2 tickets that would hit two more jackpots.

Tipton's friend, Amy Warrick—who ironically now works at a medical clinic across a busy street from the Iowa Lottery headquarters and is going by Amy Demoney—often met Tipton every week or two for food at Fuddruckers, a burger place.

The apparently soft-hearted Tipton found out that Warrick and her fiancé were having money troubles. Swell guy that he is, Tipton gave the Kansas ticket he had bought—knowing it would win—to Warrick. He told Sand he didn't plan to claim it, which made it an odd purchase in the first place. He suggested Warrick take the sure-fire ticket, win, and use the money for her wedding. He explained that he couldn't claim a big prize. He wasn't supposed to be playing at all but thought small prizes wouldn't be a problem, outside Iowa anyway. Had he been even smarter than some think he is, he also would have bought the Hot Lotto tickets in Kansas, where prizes may be claimed anonymously.

When Sand asked Tipton later if the plan was for Warrick to split the prize with him after she claimed it, he said, "Basically, yeah."

Then there was Christopher McCoulsky, a friend with whom he played "Dungeons and Dragons." Tipton dated McCoulsky's sister, "who was one of the knockout girls, you know," Tipton would recall later. No, we didn't know. But we do now, if it's relevant. "Gorgeous," Eddie added for emphasis. He took her to see the Commodores.

Tipton told McCoulsky to cash the ticket, and they would split some of the money.

eighteen

OKLAHOMA, WHERE THE CASH COMES SWEEPIN' DOWN THE PLAIN

Eleven months after buying the Hot Lotto ticket in Iowa, two $22,000 Kansas jackpot winners, six years after the Colorado drawing, and after Eddie Tipton had bought his new house with the Colorado winnings in November 2011, Tommy Tipton asked his friend, Billy Conn, to go to Oklahoma with him. While they were there, Tommy filled out Hot Lotto multi-state lottery ticket forms, then handed them to Billy, who bought the tickets at convenience stores. As luck or fixed insider jobs would have it, one of the tickets won a jackpot. Tommy called Billy and asked him to redeem the lotto ticket so Tommy's wife wouldn't find out about the money. That led to Billy's nephew, Kyle Conn, cashing the winning ticket. Both Conns got $35,000 and Tommy banked $650,000. Soon after, Eddie's bank account gained $75,000.

In an interview with Sand, Billy Conn said he was a high school graduate who worked 28 years in oil fields until he was disabled.

"How did you get into Bigfoot hunting?" Sand asked him.

Conn said his friends, "pretty serious, no bullshit guys," told him they knew something was going on in the woods. One of them had watched Bigfoot for 15 minutes. "I never believed it was there, but I knew it was there just based on what I knew," said Conn. So they decided to start hunting "these animals."

Two weeks before Hurricane Rita hit in 2005, Conn found a 42-inch dreadlock in the forest. He had it analyzed at universities and such. "The best we can come back with is it is an unknown primate. We don't know if it was Bigfoot. That's basically how I got into it," Conn said.

Conn said he got a call from Tommy Tipton in 2005, soon after the Dreadlock Find. Tipton told Conn he wanted to see the dreadlock. Conn was offshore at the time. Conn called Tipton when he was back on land. Tipton visited Conn and saw the examples. "Yeah, that's it, that's the dreadlock they have hanging off them," Tipton told Conn. They started hunting Bigfoot together using Tipton's thermal imaging equipment, which Conn found quite handy.

Conn said Tipton said he had to take some thermal gear to Oklahoma to some of his friends and asked if Conn wanted to come along.

"So I went. And we were talking about Bigfoots and stuff like that, what would happen if you get one," Conn recalled. "It would be just like winning the lottery. The conversation came around to lotteries and Tommy asked if I wanted to go in halves. I said sure. So we got to the station where we were supposed to meet the guy, and I was fixin' to use the restroom. Tommy said, 'Man, get us one of those tickets and we'll play.' I said, 'All right.' I had about forgot about it. So I went in and used the restroom and picked up some crackers and a couple of soda waters."

Conn picked up a couple of lottery play slip forms, which allow you to pick your own numbers, and took them to the car. He handed them, and a couple of soda waters, to Tommy, who asked what numbers they should play. Conn made like a random-number generator and rattled some off. Tommy filled out the forms. Conn took them in and bought the tickets.

"We got in the car and I hand him a ticket, and we head on down the road," Conn said. "I saw another store coming up on us there, and the tickets were laying there. Tommy said, "I want to play again.""

"I went in. I don't know what I bought. Maybe another soda water, or some chips, I don't know. Same thing. He asked me for my numbers. I just rattled them off. I went in and bought tickets. And we headed on down the road. I can't remember if we stopped again. We headed home.

I never thought another thing about it until a while later. He called me one day."

"Can you meet me?" Tommy Tipton asked.

"What you got?" Conn responded.

"I need to see you," Tommy said.

"Hell, yes. What you got going?" Conn asked.

"We hit that lottery," Tipton said.

"Are you shittin' me?" Conn said.

"No, we hit it," Tipton said, trying to act as surprised as one can when the result of a drawing is rigged and victory is pretty much assured.

Conn told Tipton he couldn't redeem the ticket because he didn't want to appear to be the winner. That would cause friction with his estranged wife, with whom he had had money quarrels. Plus, Conn didn't want to lose his disability payments.

Tommy Tipton couldn't cash the tickets, for fear of his connection to Eddie—who wasn't supposed to buy tickets because he worked for MUSL. He asked if Conn knew anyone else he could trust. You know, someone familiar with the Bigfoot Hunters Code of Ethics.

"I have a couple of nephews I trust," Conn told Tommy. "They are basically my own. I raised them. I trust them more than I trust my own kids."

Tipton asked Conn to talk to Kyle, one of Conn's nephews.

"I'll do it," said Conn, helpfully.

Conn told Kyle there were "other women involved"—even though he told Sand that Kyle knew his uncle wouldn't sleep around. He said he and his partners couldn't have their names on the ticket or divorces would be coming. "He knew I wasn't into chasing women."

Conn also knew Kyle Conn wouldn't ask questions.

"If we can do it legally, we can do it," said Kyle.

"We want to make sure everything is right," Billy assured. "We don't want to get no trouble."

Billy talked to a lawyer in Oklahoma a couple of days later. The man wasn't sure about the case. So Billy talked to a second lawyer, who was going to do some research and get back to him. He didn't.

Billy Conn drove back to Texas. A couple of days later, he and Kyle visited Kyle's brother-in-law, another lawyer. There was fictitious talk of other women again. The question was whether Kyle could claim the ticket. He said they needed to check with the lottery, which they did.

"They said, 'Yeah, no problem.' So a couple of days later, Kyle and I drove up there [to Oklahoma] and claimed it," Billy Conn said.

"We were talking to Tommy and he said, 'Ok, what you do right at first is you have him pull out a bunch of cash. That way it looks like you're going crazy spending it.'

"I said, 'Shit, Tommy, most people do, you know?'" Billy said.

Kyle reported that the cash was in an account. "I said, 'Get some cash. Get $100,000.' That way, we have some cash. Go crazy a little bit.'"

(Editor's note: We have heard tell that you can have a memorable shopping spree or recreational outing in Oklahoma, Texas, or even Iowa for a lot less than $100,000. But we digress.)

You know how the money in a James Bond movie, or something like "True Lies" or "Fargo" was always in a briefcase? Well if you're going to be involved in the biggest lottery scam in U.S. history—even if you don't fully realize it—some good luggage would go a long way for money exchanges.

"Well, he gave me the $100,000 in a briefcase," recalled Billy Conn. "I took 20 [thousand dollars]. Tommy said he had something that needed taken care of. He's always got some kind of deal going. So, I give him $80,000."

Billy figured he best be buying his wife some nice things "to work on the marriage and stuff." So he did. He was fixin' to make things better.

"We talked about investing it. I wanted to invest mine in land. We have several pieces of land just for hunting. We own some. We lease some," Billy said.

Tommy called Billy one day, said Facebook was going to be sold, and it was going to a huge chance to make money. Tommy wanted to buy Facebook stock. Billy said he really doesn't play the stock market, and then did it anyway. "We went in halves," Billy recalled.

Facebook took a big dive. Kyle panicked. Tommy said they had lost their shirt, but they should stay the course and maybe the stock price would come back.

Billy decided he would sell the stock to invest in land. Tommy mentioned some land in his area that Billy could lease for a lifetime. Billy gave his proceeds from Facebook to Tommy, who took care of the land lease.

Billy bought three parcels of land and started hunting on them. "It was awesome hunting," he noted, without using the word "dreadlock."

Somebody started buying land next to Tommy's place in Texas for a hunting reserve that would charge day leases. Tommy did not like this. "He wanted to buy the property," Billy said. He didn't have enough money, so Billy bought 32.5 acres.

Tommy wanted to buy a tractor. Kyle sent the money.

Billy, still smarting from the Facebook Fiasco, tried something more traditional and perhaps more aligned with the culture of his southern roots. He bought silver and gold.

How did that go?

"I lost my ass on that," Billy reported.

Tommy offered to take Billy's remaining money from the Silver and Gold Fiasco and invest in yet another lease. Billy said fine, but he needed a copy of all these lease agreements. He didn't get them.

"He had been out in the woods. He forgot about it," Billy recalled.

Billy bought some camping supplies with the lottery winnings, and then found a used pontoon boat in the newspaper (like people did in the old days).

Kyle checked it out, and he found a property by the lake, too. Billy could just leave his boats in the marina.

"We had a deer camp. We needed to get a fish camp. So we did," Billy recalled.

"Anything I needed, I just called Kyle. He pretty much handled all my finances," Billy said.

Billy has memory problems because of injuries from a drive-by shooting in Louisiana, which left a bullet lodged in his head.

Tommy called and told Kyle that he would be getting a visit about some property he had bought.

"My wife said from the start she didn't trust Tommy," Billy said. "She liked him, but she didn't trust him. There was something there. She was leery from the first time she met Tommy."

If Tommy needed something, he would call Billy, who would contact Kyle with whatever account number Tommy provided.

Sand asked if Billy had met Eddie Tipton.

"No sir," Billy said in an interview with Sand. He also hadn't met Eddie's other brother or sister. He didn't know Robert Rhodes.

He had met Alexander Hicks and saw him three or four times before he died. "I didn't see him much at the bar. I was always in the woods."

Sand asked if Tommy had said anything about winning the lottery before. "No, sir. That was a shock, when [FBI special agent] Richard [Rennison] told me that," Billy said.

Billy didn't know anything about Eddie Tipton.

Kyle Conn also talked to Rob Sand. When the interview started, Sand asked for a bit of a bio. Grab a soda water. You are in for a treat.

Conn said he was born and raised in the east Texas woods. He hunted and fished for food when he was a kid. He went to church on Sunday morning and Sunday afternoon and on Wednesdays. "I'm just a backwoods country boy who liked to hunt and fish. We worked hard. We picked watermelon. Dad pushed to get A's."

Conn said he made the Honor Roll and the National Honor Society and attended what is now Texas State University for a year.

He supported his family, which eventually included two children, by working the oil fields. He later worked for Conn Construction, fixing hurricane damage in Houston.

One day he ran into Billy. "I was just coming from Hooters. I pulled up to talk to him, and I met [Tommy] and that was it." That was in 2008.

A few years later, he saw Tommy again while he was out hunting.

In November 2008 there were some calls between Tommy and Kyle's phone. Kyle said maybe Billy used Tommy's phone.

"How did you get tied into the lottery ticket?" Sand asked after learning of Kyle's church-going, Hooters trips, hunting prowess, and chance meetings with Tommy Tipton.

"Uncle Billy come over to my house and said he had a lottery ticket for $1.2 million. He told me that him and some girls and some guys that he had gone to high school with had went up to Oklahoma on a weekend getaway. And while they were there, he bought a lottery ticket," Kyle said. "And that the girls and the guys, each of them just rambled off a random number and gave it to him, and they won the lottery. All right, he told me that he couldn't cash it in under his name because he was up there with those girls." Billy's wife would not like that, and they were on the verge of breaking up, Billy told Kyle.

Billy asked Kyle if he would cash the ticket, if it is legal. He would be paid $35,000. An Oklahoma lawyer told Billy it was legal. Kyle talked to a lawyer, his brother-in-law, Bobby Neal, a banker, and CPA and all said it was fine if he paid taxes. A few weeks later, Kyle cashed the ticket in Oklahoma—after buying the ticket from Uncle Billy for $1—and put the prize money in a Texas bank. The money was distributed as Billy wanted, he added.

It took maybe a year to distribute the money, Kyle Conn said. In some cases, he bought gold and silver for them, $30,000 worth. He bought a pontoon boat, too, under orders from Billy. And a tractor. And land. And a fish camp. Two vehicles.

"The money was sitting in my account until Uncle Billy asked me to do something, and then I did it," Kyle explained. He thinks they spent all of it. He wasn't sure if any of the purchases were for someone other than Billy.

Kyle Conn said he didn't know Tommy Tipton was involved until a few weeks before Sand called as part of the investigation. He assumed Billy had bought the ticket. He had never met Eddie Tipton. He didn't know Robert Rhodes or Alexander Hicks or Thad Whisenant.

Sand asked if Kyle knew any other Bigfoot hunting friends of Billy.

No, he did not. Because he was like a son to Billy, Kyle had been invited multiple times to hunt the One with The Big Dreadlocks. He declined.

"I ain't sold on it, buddy," Kyle explained to Sand with a chuckle. Sand, who hasn't hunted Bigfoot a day in his life, chuckled, too. "Billy's a good hunter, but he ain't killed that mother f—er yet," Kyle explained. "But he has that damn hair that I can't explain."

He referred to the dreadlock Billy found. Three feet of horse-hair-like, dread-locky stuff that professors across Texas could say only seemed like it came from a primate. Humans are primates. Apes are primates. We're not sure if Bigfoot is officially considered a primate.

Kyle isn't quite 100 percent ready to dismiss the idea.

"When I go out to that deer camp, my gun is loaded," he says.

nineteen
RIGGING THE ODDS

Let's review. Eddie Tipton had, in effect, used computer language to cut odds that range well into the millions down to a few hundred. If all went as planned, the drawing would take place on a computer that had the code he wrote. The drawing would occur on a Wednesday or Saturday, after 8 p.m. Central Standard Time. The drawings involved occurred on three specific dates—in November, December, or May—when Eddie usually traveled to Texas on vacation.

Robert Shapiro, the first assistant attorney general from Colorado, eventually told Tipton in a proceeding that he found it "remarkable" that Tipton couldn't see that the situation was akin to "insider trading" and "playing with house money."

"You were playing with inside information that the rest of the world never got," Shapiro told Tipton.

As a result of the running of the malicious code, only a small range of combinations could be involved, allowing Tipton to predict the outcome. But remember: he only could do this once a year.

twenty
EDDIE THE INNOCENT

Until Iowa officials released video of Eddie Tipton buying tickets in Des Moines—and people recognized his voice—Tipton maintained his innocence.

Eddie Tipton's attorney, Dean Stowers of West Des Moines, Iowa, insisted in an Associated Press account that Tipton was innocent.

"There's just absolutely no evidence whatsoever that he did anything to alter the proper operations of the computers that were used to pick those numbers, absolutely no evidence. It's just all speculation," Stowers told AP.

Porter once talked to a Des Moines area lawyer who described Stowers as "a piece of work."

Tipton spent years declining interview requests. But he was quoted extensively in a Daily Beast article on July 9, 2015. By the sounds of it, Tipton was as pure as the filtered tap.

Unsurprisingly, Tipton was pulling nearly a six-figure salary, and eventually topped six figures, doing I.T. work for the Multi-State Lottery Association after 12 years on the job.

He told the Daily Beast it made no sense to think he was guilty of a crime and had somehow bilked the lottery universe. "I was not hurting for money," Tipton told a reporter. "Not hurting enough that I need to take a chance and ruin my whole life. No way."

"I have to prove that it wasn't me because whoever did it—we don't know who it is," Tipton told the Daily Beast after claiming a mystery man bought the ticket.

"I know how the game works," Tipton added. "So either I'm an incredible genius that did something stupid or I'm just plain incredibly stupid. But how can I be an incredible genius and do something stupid at the same time?"

twenty one
CLOSING IN ON THE TRUTH, ONE CALL AT A TIME

The fateful phone calls between Neubauer and Philip Johnston, detailed at the beginning of this tale, had convinced Iowa Lottery staffers that a fraud had occurred. At that point they still didn't know who bought the winning ticket in the Hot Lotto drawing or that an insider had doctored the whole thing.

After those calls, a full-fledged investigation unfolded. What follows are some of the highlights.

Iowa Lottery Vice President of Security Steve Bogle called Shaw, the New York attorney, while Shaw was driving in rural New York on December 30, 2011. Shaw had some connection to the winning ticket purchase in Iowa.

The parties exchanged pleasantries much as U.S. senators might have, back when civility was still part of Washington life.

Then Bogle tried to get down to business, but in a strongly cordial, non-threatening, and matter-of-fact tone.

"Congratulations!" Bogle told Shaw.

Shaw quickly jumped in, and the clarifications, boundaries, and astonishments began. "I am the trustee. I'm not, I am not the beneficiary," said Shaw.

Bogle remained calm, affable.

"We're just very happy that the ticket came into lottery headquarters in time to preserve the ability to award the prize," Bogle said.

As if to emphasize his detachment or lack of information—or perhaps innocence—Shaw inserted: "I was asked to participate in this only recently."

But he quickly turned his attention back to the happy thought of someone claiming one of the strangest lotto plays that most in the business had ever seen. "They were lucky I was able to get the ticket out there in time. It was a close one—two hours before the deadline," Shaw said, conjuring an image of him dabbing a sweat bead or two from his brow.

He must not have understood that U.S. lotteries, as a matter of course, investigate large prize claims that come late in the game—in this case, as the clock was running out.

Still warming up for what would amount to an interrogation, Bogle said with a chuckle he was happy the package didn't fall off a courier service conveyer belt on its way to what Shaw hoped would be a big payday.

"It's one of those stories I'll put in my memoirs," Shaw assured Bogle.

Bogle, knowing the truth was going to be a story for the ages, agreed. "I'm certain, as will many people."

Bogle and Shaw talked about meeting in early January. But Shaw, who was late to the case no matter what his role proved to be, wanted to lower expectations.

"I don't know that there is that much to talk about, but I'm glad to answer any questions you may have," Shaw told Bogle.

Throughout the call, Bogle channeled an inner calm that defied the circumstances. His even, agreeable tone made the beginning of the call sound like he and Shaw were old colleagues. They were, rather, complete strangers on opposite ends of something the state thought was suspicious.

Bogle was about to test whether Shaw was representing a previously shy but legitimate, winner or winners of a big Hot Lotto prize, or if something was seriously amiss.

"One of the things that we will need is a list of all of the members of the trust, and then we will need a list of folks, people, names and addresses, from the person who purchased the ticket until it came into your possession as a trustee, so we will be able to complete our investigation," Bogle told Shaw.

Shaw appeared to be thinking on his seat. "Alright, let me cut through that. I am acting as the trustee."

Bogle's easy path to case closure was about to have a tree dropped across it.

"The ticket was delivered to me by an attorney duly licensed to practice law in the United States," Shaw said. "He represents the person who owns the ticket. They wanted to do this anonymously. The person who purchased it does not want…"

Just as the detail got juicy, the cell signal cut out and Bogle lost contact with Shaw. Bogle called back.

Shaw continued.

"As a result, they structured this so we set up a trust. I'm the trustee. The beneficiary is a Belizian corporation."

For the first time, Bogle's voice changed, if only slightly. "Ah, I'm sorry, what kind of corporation?" Bogle asked, sounding like he was trying to stay calm.

It was a corporation set up in Belize, the Central America nation known in the United States as a prime vacation spot or retirement prospect. It is also an English-speaking nation widely known for its active drug trade and a high murder rate. Let's just say that the word "Belize" seemed out of place in a discussion of lottery operations in Iowa.

Money-laundering, perhaps? Bogle had no choice but to continue his questioning.

Shaw offered what details he could, though not the name of the person or people claiming the ticket—an absolute must for anyone to get paid a prize won in a lottery game in Iowa.

"The president of that corporation…is Philip Johnston," Shaw explained.

Could this be the Canadian lawyer Mary Neubauer and Bogle talked to 30 days before?

"The trust will distribute it to the Belizean corporation, if it is collected," Shaw noted. "That is all I know about the transaction. I don't know the identity of the person who bought the ticket or arranged to have his lawyer send me the ticket. Do you understand? You may not think it is correct, or whatever, or appropriate, but that is the way it happened."

"That will give us another trail we will have to..." Bogle said, not completing the sentence.

Shaw sounded cooperative. He said he wanted to save Bogle time. He offered to talk in person and on the phone. "The trust is a New York trust. I will be glad to give you a copy," Shaw said, helpfully.

Shaw then uttered words that would make the lottery suspicious of the whole deal:

"We believe as lawyers that the client has the right of privacy. He is not required to identify himself."

Oh yes, he is, at least in Iowa—but not in six or seven other states. He could have perhaps bought tickets in those locations without so much risk of being caught.

Had Shaw just inadvertently confirmed we were talking about a single "he" as the winner? Not a group?

Bogle could be heard breathing deeply through the phone, probably through his nose. He told Shaw that was an issue they would discuss in person. Which was "lawyerese" for, "We have a big problem."

Shaw said the lawyer representing the Belizean trust would talk.

"But I won't be able to identify the purchaser," Shaw said. "I don't even know who it is. The lawyer who contacted me, I've known [Robert Sonfield] for 30 years, and he is an outstanding person. But he does not want to be identified, I guess because he's afraid the identity of his client will be revealed.

"I will do everything I can do to cooperate with you," Shaw said as the call concluded.

He spoke of a January 9 visit, after the Iowa caucuses were over and the politicians had left. Bogle and Shaw chatted a bit about the immense relief Iowans feel after the invigorating and cherished barrage of Iowa caucus campaign stops wears on, then fades away with the caucus day's end.

But Hexham Investments Ltd. of Belize was pulling Bogle's thoughts away.

When Shaw did visit Des Moines, he was dubbed Mr. Greenjeans because of the unusual clothing he wore while in Iowa's capital city—a metropolitan area dominated by insurance, finance, suits, dresses, and nonfarm attire. Shaw supposedly bragged at a posh downtown hotel about how he held the winning ticket for the mystery unclaimed jackpot.

As the case unfolded, Strutt, the head honcho at MUSL, said his staff thought the computers that might have been tampered with were long gone, he testified in a deposition. "We didn't have the machines that were involved. They were not in our possession, so we did not look at them. And when we discovered that they continued to exist—and I thought they had been destroyed—we advised the (Iowa Division of Criminal Investigation) and they took possession of them, so we have not taken a look at those machines," Strutt said.

There were other breaks.

Looking back on the case, Sand recalled a particularly key moment when Wisconsin Lottery officials called him one day. "Guess who claimed a lottery ticket in Wisconsin," someone said. "My first two guesses were Eddie Tipton and Tommy Tipton and they said, 'No, it's Robert Rhodes.' Then they said we think we still have this computer, we're going to have it analyzed.'"

Weeks later, Sand was gazing at his computer when an email from the Wisconsin officials arrived. With an attachment.

"I opened the attachment, and instantly recognized the source code as something that was going to generate random numbers, except on certain occasions. My phone rings at the next moment. It's Wisconsin, David Maahs, the assistant attorney general who did great work on this case."

"I just sent you an email," Maahs said over the phone.

"Yeah, I know, I'm reading it," Sand responded.

"Do you hear that? I think it's the 'Hallelujah Chorus' from Handel. That is what I'm hearing right now as I'm reading this attachment," Sand said, perhaps resisting the urge to try singing in the soprano voice of a man who knew it wasn't over until the skinny guy sings.

Sand's reference to the "Hallelujah Chorus" was his informal way of saying, "We just won," or "He shoots, he scores, and that's the ballgame!"

It was an incredible moment in a case that Sand had crafted from circumstantial evidence at first.

"It was instantaneously recognizable that we had what we had been criticized for so long for not having in the first trial, which was the smoking gun. I had joked at the time of finding someone who could take that single piece of paper, fold it origami style into the shape of the gun so I could actually frame that one and put it on my wall somewhere. I haven't gotten that done yet," Sand said in an interview.

Sand struggled with what to do with the code that was found.

"Having that code was fantastic," he recalled. "It provided us with a picture into exactly what Eddie Tipton did to make those numbers fixable and predictable. But at the same time, every time you are going to try a case in court, you have to keep in mind that the more simple of a case you can present, generally speaking, the better your case is."

Rootkits and code and RNGs (random-number generators) were not the simplest of concepts to explain to a judge or jury.

"If I can present a case that shows that this guy and his buddy just happened to win six different lottery tickets, in a way, that might be a better case than providing all those tickets and the code itself. Because when you present the code itself, you are adding expert witnesses, talking about things that most people don't understand, and creating room for doubt and room for argument," Sand said.

At one point, Sand asked Kansas lottery officials for the claim files for all three tickets. One was a quick pick—the computer chose the numbers—so that ticket was quickly ruled out. The other two involved numbers chosen by the buyer. One was claimed by Tipton's friend, Amy Warrick, from Iowa. One was claimed by a man from Texas. Later, both were identified as friends of Eddie Tipton.

Jackpot! Jackpot!

"He told me the first one had been claimed or purchased in the Kansas City area, at about 6:40 at night," Sand said. "Instantly, I went back to the timeline that we had drawn up from Eddie's cell phone calls as he drove down through Kansas to Texas on that day. "I said, 'Let me guess, the other one had been claimed or purchased at about 8 p.m. in Emporia or so?' And he said, 'Yeah, how did you know?'"

Yes, that's right. Eddie had picked up a winning $16.5 million ticket in Iowa in the early afternoon and was greedy enough to want two more $22,000 tickets three hours later in Kansas, all of it on his way back home to Texas on the only day in 2010 he could predict the numbers on his rigged machines.

twenty two
DESPERATION SETS IN

As it became clearer that the lottery investigators were closing in on the truth, Tipton and his team looked for a way out.

At one point, Julie Johnson McLean of the Davis Brown law firm offered a deal that included cash for charities. The world didn't know until a court date later that Davis Brown was to receive $500,000 if the ticket was cashed.

Molly Juffernbruch, vice president and general counsel of the Iowa Lottery in 2012, followed up what had to have been some interesting internal discussions with this letter:

Dear Ms. Johnson McLean:

Thank you for your offer dated January 25, 2012 concerning the payment of the Hot Lotto jackpot-winning ticket. The offer is a laudable and creative attempt to resolve this dilemma. Unfortunately, the Iowa Lottery must decline your offer, however, as we continue to have concerns about the legality of the purchase, possession, and presentation of this ticket, as required by the Iowa Code and Administrative Rules.

As our Vice President of Security Steve Bogle has previously stated, he cannot recommend the payment of the ticket to any party until he has knowledge of the name, birthdate and contact information for each person who purchased or possessed the ticket. Again, we request this information by 3 p.m. CST on Friday, January 27, 2012. Thank you for your consideration.

Regards,

Molly Juffernbruch
Vice President, General Counsel

So that didn't go well for the prize-claimers, or Davis Brown, which was brought into a controversial case.

Eventually, Shaw, who had been hounded by reporters, decided to give up the jackpot *without the consent* of Sonheim, Rhodes, or anyone else. We wish we could have been in on THAT call, when the guys from Texas heard the news.

Johnston, the man who lied to authorities and prompted a fraud investigation, and who was listed as president of a trust in Belize that Eddie Tipton tried to hide behind, later cut a deal with investigators. So did Crawford Shaw, who had tried to claim the jackpot through two local lawyers two hours before the deadline.

Johnston and Shaw identified Robert Rhodes, Eddie Tipton's pal, as the holder of the ticket in negotiations that spanned 2013 and 2014.

With the ticket nearly set to expire, lawyers called the Iowa Lottery and said they were coming in.

"Here's where it gets fun. We're now at the end of December and it's two days before the ticket is set to expire," Rich said. "We get a call from a local lawyer, who is reputable in Des Moines, saying, 'We have the ticket, we're coming in to claim it and we expect our money.'

"The interesting piece we found out later is that this Crawford Shaw who was sending the ticket was offered $500,000 from some unknown person that was going to claim the prize, as was the local law firm.

"We waited patiently, knowing it was coming. It was now Thursday [deadline day], 10 or 11 o'clock. What we found out later was Mr. Shaw sent the ticket FedEx on Wednesday and it arrived at 11:30 on December 29. This was between Christmas and New Year's. Can you imagine if the receptionist, who probably was a backup, getting the ticket worth $16.5 million and, not knowing what it was, setting it aside?" Rich said.

The ticket was in hand in Des Moines six hours before it would expire. By the time the slip of paper at issue arrived at Iowa Lottery headquarters, less than one hour and 50 minutes was left to claim the prize. The Davis Brown attorneys were on the job.

"We want the money," they told lottery officials. Lottery officials, hoping for a good outcome to a wild ride, called reporters and said a big announcement was coming.

Rich asked the two lawyers to meet the press with him. He asked for the ticket, held it, and showed it to the cameras.

Rich quickly assembled the state attorneys and they decided not to provide the money until they could confirm who bought the ticket and whether it was possessed legally.

Eddie Tipton was sitting somewhere thinking, "This is crazy." Tipton had told his representatives not to claim the prize at the last minute because that type of thing makes lottery officials suspicious.

"We decided to challenge the ticket," Rich recalled.

Initially, lottery officials said they would consider awarding the prize if Crawford Shaw showed up. Rich knew that if Shaw or Johnston showed up, the plan was to arrest them on the spot.

Shaw worked with the lottery to ensure he wouldn't be arrested. "I think he felt, 'The old hayseeds, they'll just pay it,'" Rich said.

twenty three
KANSAS SUES

As the investigation continued through the years, more evidence was uncovered in other states. By December 2015, the criminal charges against Eddie Tipton had been expanded to involve lottery prizes in Colorado, Iowa, Kansas, Oklahoma, and Wisconsin.

"Hot Lotto drawing cheat charged with rigging more jackpots," reported the Lottery Post. Eddie Tipton bonded out of jail in Iowa after being charged with ongoing criminal conduct involving the lottery wins in other states. He vowed to fight the charges.

Kansas lottery players questioned the integrity of games there.

After authorities discovered Tipton could have altered random-number generators in numerous states, Kansas filed a lawsuit in 2017.

Tipton, Kansas authorities alleged, had bought two winning 2x2 tickets in Kansas and had two friends redeem them. He bought both tickets for the drawing on December 29, 2010. That was obviously the same date and involved the same random-number generator used in the now-infamous Hot Lotto drawing.

Was he a bit greedy after winning $16.5 million?

Eddie Tipton now had left a trail that would prompt Iowa Lottery officials to nickname the scam after Interstate 35.

Some highways, like Route 66, receive references in famous jazz songs. Interstate 35 gets comments about human trafficking, lanes clogged with trucks, rest-stop romances, and grand allusions to the lottery-ticket buying habits of a man who wasn't supposed to buy any in the first place but chose to rig the ones he did.

The Iowa Division of Criminal Investigation followed Tipton's path on December 23, 2010 using records of the pings to his cell phone. He ultimately traveled from his grand estate on the south side of the Des Moines area 20 miles north to the convenience store, then south three hours to Kansas. All the while, he was calling his friend Robert Rhodes, chatting like a school kid.

Tipton picked his own numbers for both Kansas tickets, rather than allowing the computer to choose. Each ticket won $22,004. Tipton got $6,000 from a friend who claimed one of the prizes and $8,000 from the other.

twenty four
EDDIE THE GUILTY

Since that news conference in 2012 when Rich effectively declared everything over, the state of Iowa had strung together a case against Tipton and his accomplices piece by piece. It was about a year after Tipton bought the Hot Lotto tickets in Des Moines.

Tipton later said he feared Iowa because he knew the lottery's investigators were former law enforcement officials. He decided to play—or have others play for him—in other states, but in the end got greedy and played in Iowa, his home state, where he was banned from playing anyway.

The Iowa Lottery investigators believed it would be virtually impossible to rig the system so a customer could ask for a quick pick—allowing the computer to draw the numbers—and win.

The Iowa investigative crew that Eddie Tipton had feared due to its law enforcement prowess knew that the only way to cheat the system would be to submit a "manual pick"—to present the numbers on a written slip. That's just what Eddie and his gang had done. So the investigators looked into manual plays only, not the quick pick winners.

It was a case that tested souls. For months—years, really—it appeared to go nowhere, even in the hands of talented staffs of the Iowa attorney general and the Iowa Lottery.

Rob Sand vividly recalled the day his colleague, Thomas H. Miller, who was getting ready to retire, strolled over to Sand's cubicle in a state office building in Des Moines. He handed Sand an accordion file and said, "Here. Lottery case is all yours."

This was some sort of legal-world hot-potato game that Sand didn't find amusing.

"It was a case at the time that everyone looked at as sort of an interesting mystery, but it probably wasn't going to go anywhere and probably wasn't going to uncover criminal behavior," Sand said. "It was something where we needed to knock out all the leads that we had and be able to say we have done everything we can do with this, and wherever that was going to take us, which we thought was nowhere, we needed to get to nowhere."

Sand almost immediately thought about releasing the video of the shadowy, big figure buying the ticket at the Des Moines convenience store. That was the only thing Sand could think of, the only major step that hadn't been taken. He wasn't second-guessing Miller, whose career and judgment seemed almost legendary in Iowa, or others for their decision not to release the video before they checked the leads they had.

"Tom [H. Miller, no relation to Iowa Attorney General Tom Miller] had been up to Canada; he had spoken to Philip Johnston," Sand said. "He had been down to Texas and to try to talk to Robert Rhodes and his attorney, Robert Sonfield, and nothing had come of that. I think he had had a conversation with Crawford Shaw in New York. It wasn't a situation where there were a lot of dots left to connect. We simply had to find more dots.

"They had done almost everything other than follow up a couple of minor leads and then release the video," Sand said. "So that is what I pushed for from early on."

Sand understood the drawbacks the state faced if it aired the video snippet earlier. The full video was not released.

"They had held the video back for very good reasons. You release that video, and everybody sees what the purchaser looks like, all of a sudden, you are going to have a lot of people who fit that purchaser's description coming in to say, 'That's my ticket! Pay me my $16 million.'"

An agent said he wanted to nail down a couple of things and talk to Rhodes and Sonfield before the last-ditch play of releasing the video snippets.

Eddie Tipton was interviewed by state investigators within a couple of weeks after the tape was released. The video was released on October 9, 2014, almost four years after the winning ticket was purchased in Des Moines.

Tipton provided an alibi during the interview. He said he was in Texas when someone bought the winning Hot Lotto ticket in Des Moines. "Because he was a person—finally—who would have a reason not to be disclosed as the purchaser, we decided to subpoena his bank and cell phone records to prove or disprove that alibi," Sand said. "Turns out [Tipton's alibi] was disproven. To have a provable lie will normally get you where you need to be in a criminal case. That was enough to move forward."

Eddie Tipton was in big trouble. The records showed he was in Des Moines, not Texas, and the people who thought it was Eddie in the video very well could be right. Eddie had just become the prime suspect. "Moving forward" meant making the case against the MUSL techie who had made an even bigger mistake, against all odds, you might say, by deciding to buy the tickets himself in Des Moines, even after he had avoided that same scenario in other states involved in the colossal multi-state heist that was now unraveling.

Investigators worked feverishly for several months to pin down Tipton's role in the scam. Sand would note later that a couple of things slowed the pace, though it was still relatively quick.

First, no one could spend all their time chasing Eddie Tipton's past; they had other cases to work. And it took time to compile the evidence involved. It could take two to six weeks to get a requested bank record, for example.

While investigators waited for documents, they kept working the case. "We did find early on that Tipton and Rhodes had been at the University of Houston at the same time. Shortly after that, just perusing LinkedIn, we saw that they had worked together at Rhodes' old company," Rich said.

Rich was surprised that social media and cell phone records and contacts are some of the first things investigators look at in criminal cases.

This might have been a time when investigators, whatever their propensity for lawyerly decorum and straight faces, might have shown some emotion—perhaps a smile that could at least be detected by an electron microscope.

"Once we had that, we essentially knew we had our man," Sand said.

Eddie Tipton, the high-roller with the lapse of judgment, was on his way to getting his name in print. It was at the top of court documents, under the unflattering label of "defendant," and in countless newspaper stories that would suggest he was less than a model citizen.

But there was still work to do, Sand said. "We knew we would need more to put a case together, but we knew where to direct our efforts."

The identification of Tipton, the proof he was in Des Moines on the day the tickets were purchased, and his connection to Rhodes seemed to set up at least a fraud case, Sand said.

"We didn't think that was enough to necessarily prove that he fixed the ticket." Sand and other investigators wanted to pursue that more and see if Rhodes would cooperate in the case.

The identification of Tipton "unleashed a whole new universe in the case," Sand said. It prompted new questions, such as:

— What is a MUSL? How is it related to the Iowa Lottery?

— What was Eddie Tipton's job? What exactly did he do?

"If you looked at (MUSL's) website, it just said he was a security officer who just performed security consulting. Never in his interview nor in his job description would you see that he actually wrote the code for the program, which was kind of an important piece of information that was left out until a little bit later on," Sand said.

twenty five

JOHNSTON AGREES TO AN INTERVIEW IN QUEBEC

As we mentioned in the beginning of this book, things started smelling in November 2011 when Neubauer caught Johnston in a lie. He claimed to have bought the ticket, but he wasn't wearing the right attire, wasn't the right age bracket, and was in a different weight division than the man on the security video from the convenience store.

Philip Johnston had claimed In 2011 that he personally bought the ticket at the Des Moines convenience store, then, a month later, admitted he hadn't. He had refused to identify his client who did. Eventually, he agreed to a 2013 interview in Quebec City, Canada.

Johnston told investigators he had been contacted on October 17, 2011, by lawyer Robert Sonfield and his client, Robert Rhodes, both of Houston. They wanted him to help them claim a lottery prize, according to Iowa documents related to Rhodes' case. Johnston had done business with the two men previously. The two told Johnston they were representing a client who declined to be identified but wanted his prize.

So, for those keeping score, that means men from Houston, New York City, and Quebec—which along with the Belize trust added the international crime flavor to the case—had all said they represented the mystery man in the grainy video from the convenience store most likely known more for its hot dog rollers and fresh rolls and donuts than for intriguing criminal cases.

Sonfield had originally contacted Shaw about collecting the prize and had sent Shaw the $16.5 million slip of paper via Federal Express. Shaw and Johnston worked the paperwork for Sonfield and Rhodes before Shaw withdrew the claim in January 2012.

Iowa investigators interviewed Philip Johnston in August 2013. Miller found the trip to Quebec "fascinating." He had not been there before. But there was a downside: "I learned that you really can't get a good Cuban cigar for less than $40."

But back to the case.

Did someone at about this time get word to Eddie Tipton? It turns out that he convinced his boss, Strutt, it was time to "get new computers to draw the games," to wipe the old ones, which happened to contain his fraudulent code, to industry standards, and rebuild the MUSL draw computers for use beginning in October 2013, two months after Johnston was interviewed. In the mid-2000s, Tipton had gone so far as to ask the MUSL board to use computers to draw winning numbers for the hallmark Powerball game to save labor and money, but the board rejected the idea, Rich said.

Investigators interviewed Shaw in April 2014. Shaw confirmed he had a professional relationship with Sonfield for over 30 years. Shaw and Philip Johnston, at the direction of Sonfield and Rhodes, organized and completed the paperwork necessary to attempt the claim of the $16.5 million Hot Lotto ticket, according to the Iowa Division of Criminal Investigation.

That same month, Eddie's boss, Ed Stefan, quit his job at MUSL to focus on "black box" technology for lottery security systems to be able to issue lotto tickets on non-secure paper.

With evidence that Texas was important to the case, Iowa agents traveled to Houston in June 2014 to try to talk to Sonfield and Rhodes about the ticket and the mystery buyer. Sonfield and Rhodes failed to answer a whole slew of calls and messages.

On October 9, 2014, the video of the lottery ticket transaction was released, prompting multiple reports that it appeared to be Eddie Tipton. By this time, Thomas H. Miller had retired as the lead prosecutor and Sand was now on the case.

At about the same time, Porter and Rich found the previous work relationship between Tipton and Rhodes, who praised Tipton on social media as being "very focused on the bottom line."

"I would work with Eddie again in a second!" Rhodes assured readers.

With that tie made, the Iowa Division of Criminal Investigation, along with Rob Sand, used cell phone records and social media entries to round out what they needed to go after Tipton and Rhodes.

The initial charges of two counts of fraud relating to the Iowa prize were filed against Tipton on January 15, 2015, and against Rhodes three months later.

In Tipton's first trial, defense attorneys hammered the state for what they considered a lack of evidence, Sand recalled. "It was a lack of direct evidence. We didn't have a lot of direct evidence that he had fixed it. We had a very strong circumstantial case," Sand explained.

"CBS This Morning" featured an expert who scolded Sand's team for lacking direct evidence.

Remember that Tipton had said he was in Houston visiting family when the ticket was purchased. But that was a lie.

Investigators had shown through cell phone records that Tipton was in Des Moines when the Hot Lotto ticket was purchased. A photographer working for the state of Iowa analyzed the security video from the convenience store and noted that the vehicle the person drove away from the store was a light-colored crossover of some sort. Other records showed Tipton had rented a silver 2007 Ford Edge crossover on December 22, 2010. He returned it to the car-rental company on January 3, 2011.

Investigators asked Tipton about who else he might have had contact with besides family on his Houston trip. He didn't mention Rhodes but his cell phone records showed frequent and lengthy calls between the two the day the winning ticket was purchased and on other occasions.

Sand said direct evidence wasn't needed. "You didn't really need that because of the circumstances surrounding the fix. It's overwhelming evidence to look at that and say, what reasonable person would really think that the guy whose job it is to write the program, who has access to the machine at all hours, who has the ability to write a rootkit, who has the knowledge of how to install it, and the opportunity to install it, would just so happen to purchase the winning ticket?" Sand said.

"And it would just so happen to be a record jackpot. And it would just so happen to be the largest game MUSL runs, run by a [random-number generator], and just so happened to have that ticket wind up in this guy's best friend's hands. There are just too many coincidences for someone to sit there and say, 'Yeah, it's reasonable to think that he didn't fix that outcome.' A reasonable person wouldn't say that. And that's our standard," Sand said.

Sand was confident all along that Tipton would be convicted after testimony identifying him, despite a lack of direct evidence.

Iowa prosecutors knew that they had 90 days after the charges were filed to give Tipton a speedy trial. Sand said they continued to work the case with witnesses from all over the country while they built the basics around the Iowa ticket. They made sure they could show he bought the ticket and fixed the outcome.

Tipton ended up waiving his right to a speedy trial because the court wasn't buying Tipton's efforts to exclude dozens of pieces of evidence. Then he reasserted his right to a speedy trial so the prosecutors couldn't delay the trial.

Sometimes, there's nothing like a deadline to focus one's mind and to force a specific plan.

"We hit the point where we had to focus on what I like to say is 'shooting the alligator closest to the boat.' We knew we had this Iowa ticket. We knew we had to investigate this," Sand said.

But Sand and his team suspected that Tipton's crimes didn't start and end with the Des Moines convenience store purchase.

"There were reasons to think that he had fixed other tickets," Sand said. "Very unusual that you could catch someone on their first try. Why is he demanding a speedy trial? Maybe he wants to limit our ability to investigate," Sand said.

During Eddie Tipton's first trial, Stowers brought Tommy in as a character witness for Eddie. They were both characters.

It was during that July 2015 testimony that Tommy famously said the ticket buyer at the convenience store couldn't be Eddie because he wouldn't buy hot dogs.

"The person in the video also was buying hot dogs. Eddie's not a hot dog guy." Tommy Tipton testified.

"That little bit of testimony got picked up by media all over because, how weird is that?" Neubauer said.

It was such an odd statement that media reports detailing the testimony were carried all over, including in Tommy Tipton's home town of Flatonia, Texas. That's where an FBI agent who had been looking into Tommy's possible money laundering read the article and connected Tommy with his lottery-fixing brother Eddie all the way up in Iowa.

An FBI agent down South recalled that Tommy Tipton had mentioned that he claimed a portion of a $4.8 million lottery jackpot in Colorado with a payout of $568,990. The ticket was purchased on November 23, 2005.

The agent called his Iowa colleagues.

Caller: "Did you try that lottery case against Eddie Tipton?"

Sand: "Yes I did."

Caller: "Did you know Eddie Tipton's brother won the lottery, oh, maybe 10 years or so ago, somewhere out west, maybe Colorado?"

Sand: "I did not. Thank you very much for that information."

"That helped us jump start the rest of our investigation," Sand said.

If they could confirm the Colorado case, other lotteries wouldn't be able to put them off, Sand recalled. Wisconsin found a ticket tied to Robert Rhodes. Officials also found the doctored computer in storage in that state, fresh as could be.

In October 2015, Sand and Porter would cross-reference thousands of lottery winners provided by all but two MUSL states with names and numbers in the three suspects' cell phones. They found five jackpots within the group. This case was going national in a big way.

The case got away from Eddie Tipton because people often don't realize they can't control every variable, Sand said.

In December 2015, Cam Coppess, who had become vice president of security for the Iowa Lottery after Bogle retired, asked for a map of the ticket purchases and lottery wins to look for similarities. Coppess had spent 29 years on the West Des Moines police force as an investigator. He

Investigator's map of jackpots won by the Tipton "friends and family".
Source: Iowa Lottery

considered detective work—"looking under the rug to see what's there"—to be a central part of his work through the years. Coppess retired as a captain before joining the Lottery. He had worked in cyber-crime cases.

Why the map?

"Some of us are visual learners, but also it's like you are a hunter and you are trailing your game, so if you can see the game's path you can get out in front of the game's path," Coppess said in an archive interview by the Lottery. "You can see where they are going and if you can create some kind of logic, you can get out in front. All good hunters need to be in front of the game to wait for them to come into the trap. That's the way I think. The map helped me visualize what this person might be doing, because I wasn't in Tipton's head. I had never met Eddie Tipton."

When the jackpots were mapped and dated, Coppess noted it looked like an I-35 caper. Porter spotted that some of the prize drawings involved the same dates.

"In that meeting, both Rob [Porter] and Rich said, 'Oh my God!' What they saw was of the five dates they mapped, three were one date, and two were another date, though they were different years," Coppess said. "The pattern they saw based on their knowledge of the case was that the person who set up this fraud had set in the computer code certain dates that this would work on. They identified the dates."

Coppess knew how hard it was to find code on computers. But having the dates "gave them a spotlight on what to look for. Imagine looking for a needle in a haystack but now having that needle glow or you're given a magnet; that's kind of how this worked."

Sand contacted his peers in Wisconsin, who had been looking, unsuccessfully, for evidence on the computer in storage. Within hours after Sand passed along the dates that the jackpots had in common, Wisconsin authorities had found Tipton's malicious code in the computer. It was December 2015.

Wisconsin was the only state, Porter recalled, that prosecutors knew still had a random-number generator linked to the disputed jackpot. "Once we had found the trend of November and December dates being similar, we gave that information to forensic examiners who were very quickly able to find those dates in the code and unravel how Eddie Tipton committed the fraud. So it truly took a bit of information from everywhere, a team effort, to get to where we did," Porter said.

"That was a big break," Rich noted.

"I believe what Eddie Tipton did was write a simple computer code with an 'if, then' statement," Coppess said. "If it's on these dates, then give out these possibilities of numbers. The people involved in the case said that somehow the person who did this beat the random-number generator. I would suggest that he never beat it; he turned it off. It was because of his insider access to the computer and the code that he could write that 'if, then' statement.

"From a computer programmer's point of view, 'if, then' statements are about as simple of a theory or a way of working as anything. So the question that gets posed is, 'Was Eddie Tipton a really brilliant guy?' Well, he is a smart guy, but most of us learned about 'if, then' statements in our high school algebra or geometry classes. Sometimes the simpler something is, the more we overlook it. In this case, looking back—me being the guy with hindsight, that luxury—I don't think Eddie Tipton did anything too complex, but he had all this access and others trusted him. Ultimately, that's what it came down to: Eddie Tipton broke the trust of all these people who allowed him in and sought him as a content expert in the lottery world. We will have those challenges going forward, because someone else will think they can pull one over on us. Let's set up processes where we can catch them sooner than later, but don't let our guard down and think nobody will try this fraud or another fraud in the future," Coppess said.

Soon after the Wisconsin folks found the code, Rhodes cut a deal with investigators.

"Eddie Tipton is a very smart man," Sand said. "I think he felt that he could plan this out and do it, and as long as he did it just right, he would never get caught. I don't think he was prepared for that machine to be sitting in storage [in Wisconsin].

"I don't think Eddie Tipton was prepared for the idea that within two days of his purchase of the winning Hot Lotto ticket in Iowa, the Iowa Lottery was going to go get the video of that purchase," Sand said.

Bogle isn't part of the "Eddie is smart" crowd. "We have a joke in law enforcement that we only catch the dumb ones, and there are so many of them, we never catch the smart ones. Eddie got caught, so he can't be smart," Bogle said, shrugging his shoulders.

twenty six
THE VIEW FROM MUSL

While Iowa authorities pieced together the mystery, MUSL – Eddie Tipton's employer -- was reluctant to pursue the case, fearing lawsuits, Rich said.

But because of the Iowa investigators' actions, Charles Strutt, who ran MUSL for nearly three decades until the widening scandal over the Tipton case spread in 2015, shared his version of events with prosecutors in a deposition on April 2, 2015. That testimony offered Strutt's perspective on how the pieces of the case came together.

Part of the puzzle was figuring out whether Eddie Tipton had bought the ticket in Iowa himself at that north-side Des Moines convenience store just south of Interstate Highway 80. And what the heck: the guy was headed for Texas, so why did he buy the ticket 22.5 miles to the north his home, in the opposite direction of the Lone Star State?

Investigators asked Strutt repeatedly about Tipton's facial hair habits, and Strutt struggled to remember what Tipton, his colleague at MUSL, was wearing on his face five years earlier. Strutt had worked at the organization since December 1988. He could remember a lot of career highlights, no doubt. Tipton's face apparently wasn't among them.

"Do you know if Mr. Tipton had any facial hair in December of 2010?" Eddie Tipton's attorney, Dean Stowers asked Strutt.

"At some point around there, a bunch of people were growing beards," Strutt said. "I think he was one of those that attempted to grow it, but I don't think he was very successful at it, if I recall."

Strutt and Dean Stowers went back and forth and it became clear that Strutt wasn't sure just by looking at him that the figure in the video and still images that investigators had from the convenience store was Tipton. It was hard to tell if he had a beard. He was wearing clothes Tipton might have worn—jeans, a dark hoodie, a ball cap under a hood. But welcome to Iowa; that could have been a lot of people's clothing choice. But the general weight class of the large figure in the images seemed to fit Tipton.

But there was that something else: The ticket buyer now wrapped up in one of the biggest investigations in lottery history had, again, managed to buy the ticket at one of a handful of locations that recorded audio at the time.

And Strutt knew that voice.

"An image from a still I would say is not recognizable," Strutt told Assistant Attorney General Rob Sand. "The video is, to me, is quite recognizable."

Really? How so? Sand asked in so many words.

"In the video, it's his voice," Strutt said.

We're not talking about a 1 in 10.9 million chance Strutt was right. Those were the odds of someone winning Hot Lotto, assuming they didn't happen to be an I.T. worker who knew how to rig the system.

Strutt was sure this was his former colleague, Eddie Tipton.

"It is his voice. It's his mannerisms, the words that he uses, the way he speaks, the way he moves, sways back and forth, the way he reaches into his pocket. Having known Eddie for 12 years, [I can say] that's Eddie," Strutt testified.

Strutt had watched the video a dozen times when it first became available. Sand wondered why he chose to replay it so much. Strutt told him he was trying to soak it all in.

"Initially it was a state of disbelief, and then I began to display it to members of my board of directors, just [to] ask if they recognize[d] anybody in this video."

Two of those people were MUSL Board President Rose Hudson, president and CEO of the Louisiana Lottery (the same state that, in the 1800s, had corruption that shut down the entire lottery industry for nearly a century) and James Haynes, who Strutt identified as the former director of the Nebraska Lottery and chairman of the MUSL security integrity committee—and a former police officer.

Hudson called Strutt back quickly and told him to suspend Tipton. She thought the video showed Eddie Tipton.

Haynes was flying back to town on that Friday in November 2014 and hoped to watch the video the next day. "He called back immediately to say, 'Oh my God, that's Eddie Tipton,'" Strutt said in his deposition. Some MUSL employees and Iowa Lottery employees thought the same thing.

Strutt, at first, had discounted some chatter that the 50 or 60 leads the Iowa Division of Criminal Investigation received after releasing the video included a few people who thought it was Tipton. Basically, he couldn't believe Tipton would be stupid enough to buy a ticket, given the restrictions on employees. Besides, Iowa Lottery staffers were fielding all sorts of tall tales about organized crime, internet sales, clerks who supposedly stole the winning ticket, dogs who ate the homework—pretty much everything except "Bigfoot took my ticket."

Strutt testified that he asked Tipton if he was in the video. Tipton said he wasn't.

Tipton was put on administrative leave—suspended. But Strutt stayed in touch with him on security issues.

Tipton had previously been putting in 10- to 16-hour days, in part to get programming in place for two new games, Strutt said, adding that Tipton had a good work ethic. And Tipton told Strutt he really wanted to come back to work.

Strutt knew that wasn't going to happen, at least not anytime soon. Tipton's plainclothes purchase in that convenience store was a bolder move than you might think, considering ostensibly it was just a man buying lottery tickets and hot dogs.

"I mean the fact that [he was] buying a ticket, picking his numbers, using a play slip, and having those numbers [were] too many things," Strutt testified.

Strutt personally walked Tipton to the door one afternoon and told him he was being placed on leave. "Why now?" Tipton asked a confused Strutt while he was getting kicked out of his office building. It had been three years since the jackpot was won.

You have to wonder if Tipton started to panic a little bit, imagining the future if he fell into legal trouble.

Earlier in Eddie's MUSL career, a routine scan had found "malicious software"—later determined to be a relatively simple but still complicated computer code that could take control of an operating system—on one of the computers at MUSL, Strutt said. "I recall asking the questions about it and being assured it was not a wild virus on the system or malicious software. It was part of a presentation being done to other security lottery staff members."

Strutt asked Tipton about it. Tipton said not to worry, it was part of a presentation for the National Association of State and Provincial Lotteries in 2008—some seven years before trouble started to take focus in Des Moines. Strutt was assured the language wasn't infecting the system.

Hot Lotto was a game sold by multiple U.S. lotteries, which allowed them to pool the money from ticket sales to ultimately produce bigger jackpots than individual states would have been able to achieve on their own. MUSL managed the pooled money and conducted the game's twice-weekly drawings using Eddie's programmed machines.

Those four computers housing random-number generator software were locked in a plexiglass enclosure with double locks at the MUSL offices. The computers weren't hooked to the internet, and access was strictly regulated.

Even someone like Tipton wouldn't normally be in there—except to change the time on the computers, Strutt testified. Eddie did have full access to the computers to perform maintenance. Too many keys to the kingdom for easy access.

Strutt testified that Tipton probably wrote the random-number generator program in late 2005. And a lottery contractor, Gaming Laboratories International, or GLI, of Las Vegas, approved the changes when it was installed.

Strutt said nothing had turned up in the computers' automatic test runs—hundreds of them—that are intended to ensure the winning numbers selected will be random. And he noted, through questioning, that Tipton was in Texas for Christmas break on December 29, 2010.

Sand, representing the prosecution, asked Strutt if Tipton had access to the draw room for maintenance.

"The I.T. people would come in," Strutt testified. "Eddie was one of them during the time when the machine was unlocked in the presence of a draw manager and an independent auditor and on camera to make changes to the machine as needed."

But Sand noted that Tipton also had access to the machine before it was installed in the draw room. "Yes. He developed it," Strutt said.

In fact, Tipton had built random-number generators used in as many as 24 of the 36 MUSL-member states.

"Standard, if you can call a Geiger counter, those kind of things, standard," Strutt told Sand. Random-number generators were known to use Geiger counter measurements of radioactive decay, a random phenomenon, to set a "seed," or starting point.

At the time of the interview, Sand asked if the equipment involved was still in use. "Yes, they are," Strutt said.

Ultimately, Tipton was fired on January 15, 2015. It was the day he was charged with his first of two counts of fraud. That month, New Hampshire Lottery Executive Director Charlie McIntyre, the MUSL legal chair, and Rose Hudson, the MUSL board chair, hired Bill Miller, a Des Moines attorney, to protect the MUSL board interests.

In April, 2015, MUSL replaced the suspect computers Eddie had programmed at the organization's headquarters. Miller suggested no internal investigation was prudent, since the Iowa investigators were leading the investigation. Instead, a third-party company was hired to suggest I.T. vulnerabilities as a "look forward."

Thomas H. Miller, the deputy attorney general from Iowa, said Iowa investigators were dedicated to the case from the time it became clear fraud had been committed. "That was a concern to the Iowa Lottery, and thankfully so, because otherwise we never would have gotten to the bottom of this case," Thomas Miller said.

They weren't joined by lottery officials from some other states and MUSL.

"The motive to want to ignore the possibility of fraud is there and, regrettably, I believe, was there on the part of some lottery officials throughout the country who simply didn't want to hear about the possibility of any fraud in connection with their business because obviously that would have the potential of reducing business," Miller said.

Yes, an $80 billion gamble.

"Thankfully, the Iowa Lottery was run by a man who was very interested at getting to the bottom of this and letting chips fall where they may," said Miller, the deputy attorney general. "I think that is the more enlightened view in the long run of how one should approach this type of thing because confidence in the lottery ultimately rests not merely on the belief that it's being honestly run but on the knowledge that it is honestly run because there is an investigation any time there is a question of whether it is honestly run."

Miller said federal authorities in Iowa weren't interested in taking up the case. "It should [have been] a matter of national interest because [44 states and the District of Columbia each had] a lottery. This case actually did receive national attention but not near the national attention I believe it would have received if this had been an effort to defraud Connecticut or California state lotteries. It happened in flyover country."

In June 2016, U.S. Senator John Thune sent this letter to MUSL:

United States Senate

COMMITTEE ON COMMERCE, SCIENCE,
AND TRANSPORTATION

WASHINGTON, DC 20510-6125

WEBSITE: http://commerce.senate.gov

June 22, 2016

Gary Grief
President
Multi-State Lottery Association
Post Office Box 93312
Des Moines, Iowa 50393

J. Bret Toyne
Deputy Executive Director & Chief Financial Officer
Multi-State Lottery Association
4400 Northwest Urbandale Drive
Urbandale, Iowa 50322

Dear Mr. Grief & Mr. Toyne:

I am writing regarding the Multi-State Lottery Association's (MUSL) efforts to address fraud in the lottery system. In particular, I seek information regarding MUSL's efforts to protect the integrity of multi-state games such as Powerball and Hot Lotto.

Currently, 44 states, the District of Columbia, Puerto Rico, and the U.S. Virgin Islands operate lotteries.[1] In 2015, lottery ticket sales in the United States exceeded $73 billion.[2] As you know, MUSL is a non-profit government-benefit association formed in 1987 and owned and operated by member lotteries in 37 states and territories as well as the District of Columbia.[3] Each MUSL member is required to offer at least one of the games administered by MUSL and retains profits to fund projects approved by its legislature, ranging from education and health care to infrastructure improvements and tax relief.[4]

Multi-state game jackpots have soared to world record-breaking levels, dramatically increasing public interest and revenues.[5] In January 2016, the jackpot for Powerball, the top lottery game in the United States, broke the $1 billion mark for the first time ever. This $1.58 billion jackpot—the largest in history—was more than double the next largest jackpot, a 2012 Mega Millions drawing of $656 million.[6] For every $2 ticket sold, approximately 34 percent is allocated to the

---

[1] Council of State Governments, State Lotteries, http://knowledgecenter.csg.org/kc/system/files/cr_lotteries_.pdf (last visited June 22, 2016).
[2] North American Association of State & Provincial Lotteries (NASPL), Frequently Asked Questions, http://www.naspl.org/faq (last visited June 22, 2016).
[3] Multi-State Lottery Association (MUSL), http://www.musl.com (last visited June 22, 2016).
[4] Id.; see e.g., South Dakota Lottery, Where The Money Goes, http://lottery.sd.gov/about/where/ (last visited June 22, 2016).
[5] Niraj Chokshi, A Jackpot-Rigging Scandal is Forgotten as Powerball Fever Sweeps the United States, WASH. POST, Jan. 10, 2016, https://www.washingtonpost.com/news/post-nation/wp/2016/01/09/the-company-that-runs-powerball-had-a-16-5-million-jackpot-rigged-by-a-former-employee/.
[6] Ashley Southall, Powerball Has 3 Big Winners, in California, Florida and Tennessee, N.Y. TIMES, Jan. 13, 2016, http://www.nytimes.com/2016/01/14/us/numbers-chosen-for-powerball-with-biggest-jackpot-ever.html.

Mr. Gary Grief & Mr. J. Bret Toyne
June 22, 2016
Page 2

jackpot pool.[7] One estimate of more than one billion tickets sold for the record-breaking
Powerball jackpot indicates that nationwide revenues may have exceeded $2 billion.[8]

Given their popularity and the large sums of money involved, recent allegations of fraud in
multi-state lottery games raise serious concerns. According to authorities, a lottery vendor who
served as the security director for MUSL manipulated drawings by installing software code into
the random number generators used by MUSL to select winning numbers that allowed him to
"predict" winning numbers on specific days of the year.[9] Six multi-million dollar prizes have
been linked to the accused lottery vendor.[10]

In October 2015, as the scope of this jackpot-fixing scandal spread, MUSL placed Charles Strutt,
executive director since its founding, on administrative leave and relieved him of his duties.[11]
Reports indicate that the board believed new leadership would benefit the rebuilding of the
association, and Strutt's retirement became effective March 31, 2016.[12] As of the date of this
letter, I understand the search for a new executive director is still ongoing.[13]

Also in October 2015, MUSL approved a series of rule changes that make it much harder to win
the jackpot in a multi-state lottery.[14] The new rules lowered the odds of winning Powerball
jackpots from one in 175 million to one in 292 million, but improved the odds of winning
smaller prizes.[15] The rule aims to boost jackpots, which in turn increase ticket sales.[16]

Other than seeking new leadership, it is unclear what additional measures MUSL is
implementing to provide effective oversight to ensure the integrity of lottery games. Indeed,
some have suggested that the excitement about increasingly large jackpots has eclipsed reports of

---

[7] *See* Florida Lottery, http://www.flalottery.com/powerball-faq (last visited June 22, 2016).
[8] Walt Hickey, *Everyone Is Freaking Out About The $1.5 Billion Powerball, And The Stats Agree,*
FIVETHIRTYEIGHT, Jan. 12, 2016, http://fivethirtyeight.com/features/billion-dollar-powerball-lottery/.
[9] Ryan J. Foley, *Code Let Lottery Vendor Predict Winning Numbers, Police Say,* ASSOC. PRESS, Apr. 6, 2016,
http://bigstory.ap.org/article/02fd5ec67d794105a877e4d165b3b95a/lottery-insiders-brother-arrested-jackpot-fixing-
scandal.
[10] *Id.*
[11] Ryan J. Foley, *Key Lottery Leader Out Amid Jackpot-Fixing Case,* ASSOC. PRESS, Dec. 23, 2015,
https://www.yahoo.com/news/apnewsbreak-key-lottery-leader-amid-jackpot-fixing-case-181255390.html?ref=gs.
[12] Public Gaming, Lottery News,
http://www.publicgaming.com/index.php?option=com_content&view=article&id=20053:charles-chuck-strutt-has-
decided-to-retire-as-executive-director-of-the-multi-state-lottery-association-musl-effective-march-31-
2016&catid=30:us-lottery&Itemid=30 (last visited June 22, 2016).
[13] *See* Job Announcement, Exec. Dir., MUSL, http://www.musl.com/docs/MUSL_Executive_Director.pdf (last
visited June 22, 2016).
[14] Lizette Alvarez, *The Biggest Powerball Jackpot Ever: The Odds and Where the Money Goes,* N.Y. TIMES, Jan. 12,
2016, http://www.nytimes.com/2016/01/13/us/powerball-drawing-
jackpot.html?version=meter+at+12&contentId=&mediaId=&referrer=&priority=true&action=click&contentCollecti
on=U.S.&module=RelatedCoverage&region=EndOfArticle&pgtype=article.
[15] *Id.*
[16] Joseph Spector, *Odds Are, You Won't Like This Powerball Story,* USA TODAY, July 6, 2015,
http://www.usatoday.com/story/news/nation/2015/07/06/odds-are-you-wont-like-this-powerball-story/29799555/.

Mr. Gary Grief & Mr. J. Bret Toyne
June 22, 2016
Page 3

insider fraud and what MUSL is doing to address the issue.[17] Therefore, pursuant to the Committee's oversight responsibilities, please provide responses to the following:

1) How has MUSL resolved the instances of prior lottery vendor fraud? What specific fraud-reduction policies, including but not limited to enhanced security of random number generators, has MUSL implemented since the jackpot rigging scandal to ensure that competition in multi-state lotteries is free from fraud?

2) Did MUSL conduct an internal investigation of the incidents? What were the results of that investigation? Please provide any report issued.

3) How is MUSL providing assurance of the integrity of its games to consumers?

4) Does MUSL anticipate any further changes to the Powerball game rules? If so, please provide a description of any such changes.

Please provide your response as soon as possible, but by no later than July 7, 2016. In addition, please brief Committee staff on these issues by no later than July 15, 2016. If you have any questions, please contact Ashok Pinto or Peter Feldman of the Majority staff at (202) 224-1251. I appreciate your attention to this important matter.

Sincerely,

JOHN THUNE
Chairman

cc: The Honorable Bill Nelson
        Ranking Member

---

[17] *See* Chokshi, *supra* note 5.

To which the new MUSL Chair, Gary Grief, director of the Texas Lottery responded:

 **MUSL**

MULTI-STATE LOTTERY ASSOCIATION
4400 NW Urbandale Drive
Urbandale, Iowa 50322
Telephone: 515-453-1400   Fax: 515-453-1420
http://www.MUSL.com

July 7, 2016

The Honorable John Thune
Chairman
United States Senate Committee on Commerce, Science and Transportation
512 Dirksen Senate Office Building
Washington, D.C. 20510-6125

RE: Multi-State Lottery Association

Dear Chairman Thune,

Thank you for your request for information regarding the security of Multi-State Lottery Association (MUSL) lottery game drawings and also regarding the Powerball game.

Founded in 1987, MUSL is a nonprofit government benefit association owned and operated by thirty-seven (37) state and jurisdictional governmental lotteries. The MUSL Board of Directors, which oversees operations of MUSL, is comprised of the Directors and CEOs of MUSL's thirty-seven Member Lotteries. MUSL additionally has licenses with the remaining ten US state lotteries regarding the Powerball and Mega Millions lottery games.

Lottery Drawings and Security

MUSL conducts live televised ball drawings in Tallahassee, Florida for the Powerball game. MUSL also conducts random number generator (RNG) drawings from its offices in Urbandale, Iowa for the All or Nothing, 2by2 and Hot Lotto multi-jurisdictional lottery games, as well as drawings for several state lotteries' local games.

MUSL knows that the public must trust the integrity of its games, and therefore takes seriously the security of its draw processes. We continuously examine and audit our practices, policies and procedures. After the arrest of Eddie Tipton, we conducted an enhanced, rigorous, detailed, and comprehensive review of our drawing processes and procedures which employed random number generators (RNGs) for the production of drawing results. Importantly, the Tipton matter involves the only known allegations of impropriety involving MUSL or MUSL's games.

Before addressing our efforts since the Tipton arrest, please note that the integrity of the Powerball drawings have never been compromised. Drawings to determine the Powerball winning numbers do not use RNGs but are instead completed by a ball drawing conducted on live television. While an RNG is used to determine the multiplier for the Power Play add-on game to Powerball, an RNG is not used to produce the Powerball drawing results. As indicated below, we are confident that our efforts since the Tipton arrest have helped to ensure that any MUSL drawings involving use of an RNG are completed with utmost integrity.

MULTI-STATE LOTTERY ASSOCIATION

Per your request, attached is a copy of the independent investigation report prepared by MUSL's outside counsel firm Dorsey & Whitney regarding the Hot Lotto drawing at issue in relation to Tipton's original arrest. In response to the investigation's findings, MUSL took the following action to ensure that the RNG games are free from compromise:

- All RNGs used at MUSL, including those compromised by Mr. Tipton, were removed from service. RNG's associated with Mr. Tipton's conduct were provided to law enforcement and have been in the possession of Iowa criminal investigators since early 2015. New RNG's were developed by MUSL staff after Mr. Tipton's departure and do not use or rely on any RNG software developed by Mr. Tipton.

- Each step of the RNG development process was overseen by a distinct and separate MUSL Security team.

  - The RNGs are isolated (air-gapped) with no Internet connectivity or connectivity with any other internal or external network system.

  - Once an RNG is developed, both MUSL IT and Security personnel are prohibited from interacting with the RNGs without both the MUSL Draw Manager and an independent third party auditor present.

  - Any modifications require retesting and the recertification of the RNG by independent third party industry experts.

- MUSL conducted and continues to conduct detailed and rigorous monitoring of all processes, procedures, and equipment involved in lottery drawings conducted by MUSL.

- MUSL engaged several independent, industry recognized experts to specifically test and provide recommendations regarding MUSL's RNG hardware and software and evaluate the RNG development processes, drawing processes and related security. While the release of the results of these ancillary reviews could compromise the integrity and security of MUSL as the results contain confidential security-related information, we provide this listing in an effort to be as open and transparent as possible, and we welcome the opportunity to discuss these reviews with you and your staff.

  - These companies are *SeNet International, Delahanty Consulting, BMM Testlabs, and Digital Intelligence*.

  - The RNG software, hardware and the drawing room environment have been reviewed and inspected to address both randomness and security-related concerns.

- MUSL continuously conducts meticulous analyses, audits, and reviews of all MUSL lottery games using experienced career lottery professionals in the areas of security, law enforcement, information technology (IT), and audit. All MUSL employees go through a thorough background check process upon employment and periodically thereafter.

MULTI-STATE LOTTERY ASSOCIATION

- MUSL enhanced its physical security through increased use of video cameras and recordings, motion detectors, and other security measures. All of the MUSL facilities and, most importantly, the draw room itself are under constant and recorded video camera surveillance 24/7/365. The draw process requires both a draw manager and independent third party draw auditor providing oversight of the process.[1]

- MUSL has also created a dedicated, independent internal risk and assurance function that evaluates the on-going design of our safeguards and tests the effectiveness of those controls and procedures. This position reports directly to the non-executive Chairman of the Audit Committee.

The result of these efforts is that MUSL is confident that its current procedures address all known risks that lottery game drawings by MUSL can be compromised. To maintain that confidence, MUSL continues to review and monitor its activities and processes to ensure that its systems remain secure. We recognize that we must remain vigilant to prevent actions by individuals determined to cheat. As part of this process, MUSL is conducting periodic third party security reviews and implementing Board-approved recommendations. The repeated findings by independent experts confirm that MUSL lottery games and drawings are secure and free from compromise.

MUSL has responded to several state legislative requests regarding lottery integrity. State and jurisdictional lotteries are primarily responsible for communicating information to their players and their local press. We know that many of the state and jurisdictional lotteries have directly communicated with their oversight commissions and legislatures relating to these matters.

The Powerball Game

The Powerball lottery game is the best known lottery game in the world. The game was created in 1992, and has undergone matrix and odds changes roughly every three years to meet the changing demands of the players in the game. The most recent matrix and odds changes occurred in 2015, and there is no expectation that the game will require a matrix or odds change for at least two more years. Additionally there is no expectation of substantive change to the Powerball Rules that would impact how the game is played.

Notably, while the Powerball Grand Prize odds have been increased to 292 million to 1 (overall odds 24.87 to 1), these Grand Prize odds are similar to the US Mega Millions lottery game Grand Prize odds at 258 million to 1 (overall odds 14.71 to 1), and are not the largest Grand Prize odds in a lottery game in the world. For example the Italian SuperEnalotto Match 6 Jackpot odds are 622 million to 1 https://en.wikipedia.org/wiki/SuperEnalotto.

---

[1] MUSL is aware that the jackpots cited in relation to the new charges against Mr. Tipton have values of $568,990 out of a $4.5 million jackpot won in Colorado on November 23, 2005; $2 million (annuitized value - $1,147,630 paid out) won in Wisconsin on December 29, 2007; $1.2 million (annuitized value - $907,715.58 paid out) won in Oklahoma on November 2, 2011 and two $22,000 prizes won and paid out in Kansas on December 29, 2010. MUSL's efforts described above at addressing the issues apply to all MUSL drawn games.

MULTI-STATE LOTTERY ASSOCIATION

As you state in your letter, state and jurisdictional lotteries exist to provide a voluntary and valuable revenue source for those states and jurisdictions. These revenues go towards general education, environmental efforts, college scholarships, senior citizen programs, property tax relief, the general coffers or other purposes as directed by the individual state or jurisdictional lottery statutes.

So far in FY 2016, the Powerball game alone has provided over $2.3 billion in revenues to benefit the states and jurisdictions participating in that game.

We hope this information provides the additional level of assurance you seek. As requested, we will be in contact with your staff to schedule a further briefing.

Sincerely,

Gary Grief
MUSL Board President

The attachment to the letter called "The Bill Miller Report" was produced by the MUSL lawyer, who led the overview.

MEMORANDUM

TO: MUSL Board of Directors

FROM: William J. Miller

DATE: April 29, 2016

RE: Completion of Hot Lotto Draw review

I.   Nature of review.

Our law firm was retained by the MUSL Board of Directors to conduct a confidential and privileged investigation of possible fraud surrounding the Hot Lotto draw of December 29, 2010 (the "Hot Lotto Draw") and report our findings to the Board. We were asked to prepare a report in accordance with the Institute of Internal Auditors International Professional Practices Framework. The scope of the investigation was to include, but not be limited to, the following:

1.   Determining whether fraud or any other wrongdoing has occurred, including but not limited to potential manipulation of MUSL equipment or processes and prohibited play by MUSL employees;

2.   Determining if any other occurrences of fraud have occurred or if this was an isolated incident;

3.   Determining the loss or exposure associated with the fraud, including reputational loss;

4.   Determining who was involved;

5.   Determining how the fraud happened, including, but not limited to:

   a.   Identifying any control weaknesses that may have contributed to the alleged criminal activity or fraud;

   b.   Identifying any violations of policy, processes or internal controls which may have contributed to the alleged criminal activity or fraud; and

6.   Recommending any changes in policy, processes, internal controls or business practices.

To complete this work, we were assisted by a committee of MUSL directors. This Committee has acted on behalf of the MUSL Board to ensure that our firm had the resources necessary to perform its work. After initial discussion and consultation, the Committee formed a team of skilled employees of member lotteries to conduct the review and generally support our firm's efforts. The Team reflected a wide range of skills and experience and included two members with significant experience in internal controls and audit, a tenured director of information technology, and a security director with substantial law enforcement experience. Other than serving as a conduit for requests for information and making the necessary contacts to create the Team, the Committee played no role in our work, and had no input into the conclusions reached by the Team.

DORSEY & WHITNEY LLP

Throughout most of its existence, the Team met weekly or more frequently. The Team reviewed numerous documents and materials that it determined were of interest. In addition, the Team conducted multiple confidential interviews of persons identified as possibly having information relevant to the investigation. The interviews were completed over several months, with the most recent and final completed at the end of March 2016.

Every current MUSL employee and several former employees were interviewed. All MUSL employees were asked a series of questions regarding fraud and related topics consistent with internal audit standards. While in Des Moines for employee interviews, a majority of the committee viewed a drawing from start to finish to review current practices, many of which are consistent with past practices. The Team members did not identify any irregularities in this process and the several procedures that appear to ensure the security and integrity of the drawings themselves.

Unfortunately, there are gaps in information relating to the Hot Lotto Draw due to the absence of documents or other material. There was no indication that this information was unavailable due to any effort to hide the information, but instead as a result of regular/course of business practices at MUSL.

II.   Conclusions.

A. Overview. As described above, the first topic to be addressed by the Team was "[d]etermining whether fraud or any other wrongdoing has occurred, including but not limited to potential manipulation of MUSL equipment or processes and prohibited play by MUSL employees." On July 20, 2015, former MUSL employee Eddie Tipton was found guilty of fraud in relation to the Hot Lotto Draw. Additionally, Tipton and others are now charged with additional, similar crimes, some of which are pending trial in July 2016 and others that will be tried to a jury in the future.

Miller observed the entire first trial arising from the allegations against Tipton pertaining to the Hot Lotto Draw. The Team had available to it the entirety of the trial transcript as well as most of the physical evidence from the trial. In addition, the Team also had the benefit of reviewing pre-trial deposition transcripts that included information that was not admitted by the trial court for the jury's consideration. The Team gave due consideration to the jury's verdict in completing its review of this matter. Ultimately, however, the jury's verdict was based on the evidence presented at trial, and nothing reviewed by the Team disclosed material information that was not presented to the jury. In other words, the Team located no "smoking gun" otherwise overlooked by the Iowa prosecutor.

Based on the jury's verdict, the Team adopted the assumption that Tipton committed the crimes for which he was convicted, which permitted an analysis of "why did it happen" that may be more beneficial to MUSL than knowing precisely "how it was done." Further, we believe that our recommendations, delivered in a prior privileged and confidential conference with the MUSL Board, will strengthen the organization more broadly than if our focus had been based solely on what required remediation with respect to the Hot Lotto Draw.

The Team's extensive review did not locate "proof" of "fraud or any other wrongdoing" such as "manipulation" or "prohibited play." The Team's effort on this point was limited by the fact it did not have subpoena or other compulsory power and some items that might have been reviewed were not available. However, any limits on the Team's ability to do a law-enforcement style investigation must be read in context with the reality that a jury concluded that Tipton was

2

guilty of fraud in relation to the Hot Lotto Draw. In addition, based on the information gathered and reviewed, the Team found no basis to conclude that any other MUSL employee, past or present, was involved with the Hot Lotto Draw fraud for which Tipton was convicted. In other words, the available information indicates Tipton did not work with any of his co-workers to do wrong, but instead worked independently.

B.   Summary of conclusions.   As noted, the scope of the Hot Lotto Draw investigation included six general areas of inquiry, which are specifically addressed with the following conclusions:

1.   Determining whether fraud or any other wrongdoing has occurred, including but not limited to potential manipulation of MUSL equipment or processes and prohibited play by MUSL employees;

It is unclear by which metric or standard the Team could or should independently judge this point.   Notably, the Team was privy to information without the limitations of rules of evidence that restricted the evidence presented to the jury in the first Tipton case.   Nonetheless, the information available to the Team did not prove to all Team members beyond a reasonable doubt that Tipton committed the crimes with which he was charged in his first case.   Information about the second Tipton case is still developing, and trial is imminent. As noted, however, the Team believes MUSL must assume that Tipton acted in a fashion consistent with the jury's verdict in the first Tipton trial and the allegations in the second for purposes of assessing and continuing to assess MUSL operations.

2.   Determining if any other occurrences of fraud have occurred or if this was an isolated incident;

Tipton and others are presently charged with additional crimes similar to the fraud counts against Tipton in his first trial.   The Team did not substantiate any allegations with respect to the second set of Tipton charges, which remain pending and are in the province of the prosecutor and, ultimately, a new jury.   We were, unfortunately, working without complete information regarding the prosecution's new charges and, of course, without the prosecution's ability to gather information that might support the charges.   Miller continues to monitor these matters and believes additional developments may create new issues to be explored internally at MUSL.   For now, the Team believes speculation and clumsy inquiry is unwarranted and problematic.

3.   Determining the loss or exposure associated with the fraud, including reputational loss;

This item is incomplete because the Hot Lotto Draw and allegations in relation to Tipton are ongoing and continue to receive news coverage.   While it is apparent MUSL has been damaged – for instance, it has incurred legal fees and costs in responding to the Tipton cases that would not have been otherwise necessary – those damages are not complete or fully quantifiable at this time.

4.   Determining who was involved;

As noted, based on the information gathered and reviewed, the Team found no basis to conclude that any other MUSL employee, past or present, was involved with the Hot Lotto Draw.

3

In other words, the available information indicates Tipton did not work with any of his co-workers to do wrong, but instead worked independently.

    5.   Determining how the fraud happened, including, but not limited to:

          a.   Identifying any control weaknesses that may have contributed to the alleged criminal activity or fraud;

          b.   Identifying any violations of policy, processes or internal controls which may have contributed to the alleged criminal activity or fraud; and

Every "audit" or review of an organization should identify practices or procedures that can be enhanced or improved. The Hot Lotto Draw has prompted MUSL to undertake a searching review of its operations and the Team believes the organization has been bettered by this effort. Most of these efforts are security-related, and a public description would undermine their purpose and effect.

Nonetheless, the Team identified no specific MUSL practice or procedure that could or should be said to have led to or caused the activity alleged against Tipton. Tipton appears to have acted alone within MUSL with criminal intent. Like any organization, MUSL must remain cognizant of this type of threat and constantly act to avoid or neutralize the threat.

    6.   Recommending any changes in policy, processes, internal controls or business practices.

As noted, limited recommendations were provided to the Board in confidential and privileged discussions. The Team has observed recognition and implementation of its recommendations by the Board and MUSL employees. The Team encourages the Board to ask the Team or a new team to review the implementation of its recommendations in the future.

* * *

We appreciate the opportunity to be of service to the Board in the completion of the Hot Lotto Draw review. Please contact us with any questions now or in the future.

4

Note: No update had been sent to Senator Thune by the time this book went to print. The official MUSL document still stands with the sentence "The Team's extensive review did not locate "proof" of "fraud or any other wrongdoing" such as "manipulation" or "prohibited play."

twenty seven
THE CLUES PILE UP

You read in chapter one that Neubauer's conversation with Johnston had convinced the lottery folks that at least one fraud had occurred, because Johnston had lied about buying the lotto ticket in Des Moines. That set off a scramble for the truth.

Recalling the whirlwind of Iowa authorities' investigation later, Mary Neubauer, the Iowa Lottery's vice president for all things communication and external affairs, recalled how the "long, strange trip" finally crossed the finish line.

The lottery reminded the public at one month, three months, six months, nine months, and 11 months that whoever had the ticket needed to cash it out before a looming deadline.

"At that point, we were losing hope," Neubauer said. "It was possible someone lost the ticket. We were into the disappointment phase."

But they still had the video of the lotto ticket purchase.

Investigators wanted to check into all the leads before they released the video from the convenience store, because they knew that the release would probably mean a new round of people falsely claiming to be the winner. "We thought we might have a line of people out the door all dressed up as a heavyset guy wearing jeans and a hoodie trying to say they were the winner," Neubauer said.

Rich recalled that the hot breath of the statute of limitations—the deadline to file charges in the case—bore down on the investigators.

"We don't have great leads," the team acknowledged. "As a group, the decision was, last resort, let's go ahead and release the tape and see if anyone recognizes this black blob that was standing in front of the QuikTrip counter," Rich recalled.

The authorities released the security-camera video with just the part showing the purchase on October 9, 2014. "What the public doesn't know is we actually have a much longer piece of video from inside that store," Neubauer recalled. "You can see the man coming up to the counter to purchase that ticket." He bought other tickets, and hot dogs—a seeming simple snack that would propel the case to the national stage later.

Eddie paid the Des Moines convenience store with a $50 bill. Later, in court, it would be revealed that Tipton had shopped at Jordan Creek Town Center—the area's largest and newest mall—at 12:41 p.m. He got $100 in change. He had talked to Rhodes for 71 minutes, beginning at 8:53 a.m. But the next time they talked was at 7:19 p.m., Tipton was in Gardner, Kansas, outside Kansas City.

The store video shows Tipton walking outside to a car after buying his tickets and hot dogs. It's kind of fuzzy the further he gets outside the store, but you can see clearly enough that he pulled the sweatshirt hood down off his head, he took off the hat, and he got into a vehicle.

"The fact that he walked outside and immediately took off the hoodie and that hat says to me that he clearly didn't want the camera to see who he was," Neubauer said.

"He got into what appeared to be small SUV. We did freeze frames on the video."

The camera couldn't make out the license plate. But the SUV appeared to be a white or silver model, and they got a good look at the front grill.

Rumors flew that the scam was an inside job, but others had all kinds of wild theories of outside jobs. One man thought the figure on the video might be his deceased friend and offered to go to the junkyard to search vehicle wreckage. Some thought someone from the post office over on Des

Moines' Second Avenue might have won, or perhaps someone stole the ticket, killed the purchaser, and threw the body in the Des Moines River.

"There were all kinds of wild stories," Neubauer recalled. Three hundred tips came in through Survey Monkey.

twenty eight
WORKING THE CASE

Bogle began work at the Lottery in 2011 after his predecessor resigned. He was tough on investigators, who upped their game, improved their techniques, and expressed great respect for him. They would be tested by more than Bogle. They now faced a bizarre case unlike any other.

In Tipton's statement to prosecutors after the case, he noted that at the time he knew Rich and the Iowa Lottery team were sniffing around, had video, and that the winning Hot Lotto ticket had not been presented to claim the prize.

"The claim had not been made," Tipton recalled in his interview with prosecutors. "The ticket was still out in the wind."

Sand asked Tipton if he was wearing the hoodie to shield himself from the camera.

"No. It was cold," Tipton said. He didn't remember if he wore a hat, or a beard or stubble.

Tipton might have gotten away with the scheme but for the checks and balances the Iowa Lottery had in its system. Basically, Eddie could create a random set of numbers, and predict a small set of probable winners, but he couldn't create his own ticket. He had to buy it at an Iowa lottery retailer. And it was unfortunate for him, and ended up being a godsend for investigators, that Eddie Tipton—rather than choosing a different store, buying a ticket in a state that would let him be anonymous, or perhaps sending a friend to make the buy—picked one of only four Iowa retailers that at that time recorded purchases with both video and sound. There were nearly 2,400 others that didn't.

Eddie Tipton's voice, recorded by the camera system, gave him away later.

But for this moment, Tipton's voice instructed Rhodes to do whatever Rhodes wanted.

twenty nine
IOWA 'HAYSEEDS' DON'T BUY THE LIE

As the investigation continued, the case created a near-sellout of animal excrement detectors. Johnston's lie about buying the ticket had led to discussions of various ways to redeem the prize—still without identifying the winner. Iowa authorities continued to say that wasn't possible.

"You had the lying lawyer in Canada, who then, after Crawford Shaw comes forward, the lying lawyer from Canada is listed as an officer for some corporation in Belize that doesn't exist. I mean it's like, 'Really guys, you want us to believe this?'" Rich recalled. "I think they thought they were coming to Iowa, and they were going to deal with a couple of hayseeds, and their big New York lawyer would come in here and roll over us. And we'd say, 'Oh, yes sir, let me write the check for you right now.'"

Shaw traveled to Iowa. He claimed he didn't know who bought the ticket. It was during his stay in a swanky Des Moines hotel that he became known as Mr. Greenjeans.

The press was hanging out at Shaw's home doorstep. He had to disconnect his cell phone. It was all so strange. Something was amiss.

"The pressure finally got to him, and he got with the local lawyers and said, 'Let's figure something out,'" Rich added.

That's where the plan to give half to charity emerged, but Tipton would have pocketed about the same amount due to tax implications. "We saw through that right away," Rich said.

The Iowa legal team huddled to figure out how to end the case without years in court. They told Rich the call was his.

"Why don't we call their bluff?" Rich said. "Let's say we need the ID by Friday or we aren't going to pay the ticket. Let's see if we can get them to blink. So we set a deadline for Friday at 3 p.m., that they either told us [who bought the ticket] or we weren't paying. We publicly stated that in the press not knowing what might happen.

"We got a call on Thursday saying, 'We are going to withdraw the claim. We just don't want the publicity. The person has too much money and it just isn't something they want.'"

At this point, Rich and his team knew that the saga ran from Canada to New York to Belize. "It just stunk to high heaven," Rich summarized.

About 5 p.m. that Thursday—January 26, 2012—Tipton's three lawyers walked into Rich's office.

"We cordially said, 'How are you doing?' and talked about the weather," Rich recalled.

"We were dying inside, thinking, 'Is this really going to happen?'"

The lawyers said they had something for the lottery. They presented documents withdrawing the prize claim. "And we said, well thank you very much. Have a nice day."

But when the lawyers left the office under escort (as all visitors to the lottery do), the scene changed dramatically.

"Everybody went absolutely nuts. We were screaming. We were cheering," Rich said. "Because this would give us some certainty that what we felt we knew was really there."

Rich walked downstairs to meet the local press, with AP and U.S. News & World Report and other national reporters via a phone link, at the news conference.

"We kind of said, "Can you believe it? What the hell? They withdrew the claim!" Rich recalled. At the same time, an investigation was announced.

The work of sifting through claims of mafia involvement and tales taller than Eddie Tipton continued.

"We knew it was either someone who knew they would be arrested if they claimed it, who had had problems with the law, or it might have been an internet buy. Under Iowa law, you can't buy in Europe (or Canada), a ticket for Iowa. You have to buy it in Iowa," Rich said.

thirty
"THAT'S EDDIE TIPTON!"

When the video came out, Neubauer and officials at the DCI got the same message from multiple people: "That's Eddie Tipton!"

Iowa Lottery officials got several tips on October 10, 2014, that the man in the video "sounds like" Eddie Tipton. And on October 14, Strutt got a call from a MUSL-member employee, Michael Boardman of the Maine Lottery, identifying the person in the video as Tipton.

Jobes, the assistant Iowa DCI director, recalled the reaction among DCI agents working the case. "I seem to recall some sense of surprise, I guess, of where this was now pointing back to. That was someone on the inside, so to speak, who knew they weren't supposed to be playing, who was prohibited from playing and had sort of been operating in our own backyard all this time," Jobes said in the Lottery's archive video.

"We were taken aback, because that clearly is someone who [worked] in the lottery industry and you never want to think something like this would be a case of insider fraud," Neubauer said.

But in addition to the call from the Maine Lottery staffer, an Iowa Lottery employee also called investigators and said she thought the person in the video was Eddie Tipton. "They both said even though they couldn't quite see the face of the person on the security camera, the voice they were completely convinced was Eddie Tipton's," Neubauer added.

Neubauer makes a living spreading the word about lottery games, staging news conferences for winners, and warning people not to gamble too much. As was the case with the entire lottery world, she had never seen anything like this.

The reality that this might have been an inside job started to settle in. "The investigation began in earnest into: Could it have been Eddie Tipton? It was pretty quickly determined that it could have been Eddie Tipton," Neubauer said.

Tipton needed an alibi that had better odds of success than your average, legally handled Hot Lotto ticket. He told officials he was out of town the day the someone bought the ticket. Which might have been a fine alibi, had it been true.

Unfortunately for the "I was in Texas for the holiday" school of innocence, state investigators went after Eddie Tipton's cell phone records, as well as those of Tommy Tipton and Robert Rhodes.

And there it was: Evidence that Tipton had, in fact, used his cell phone in the Des Moines area near the time the "winning" ticket was purchased on the north edge of town. They also found that Tipton had rented a small white SUV for his drive to Texas that day. The freeze frame of the front grill of the SUV from the security camera footage at the north Des Moines store matched the make and model of the SUV he had rented.

"A lot of things lined up to indicate that it was Eddie Tipton," Neubauer said.

Soon after, the authorities arrested Tipton, who in their view was the shadowy ticket buyer in the hoodie, ball cap, and jeans at the Des Moines convenience store, speaking in a relatively forceful voice that was picked up on the video feed.

"For the rest of us at the lottery that was just a real stab to the heart… to know that it appeared to be someone in [our] industry who had done that," Neubauer said. He was a man who worked for MUSL to make sure the systems were secure and couldn't be cheated.

"If it was Eddie Tipton, that would be a real abuse of power and a true betrayal to the lottery industry. That was a horrible thought. Ultimately, he was convicted, and eventually, he confessed to the crime

Defense lawyer Dean Stowers, left, reacts as he and his client, Eddie Tipton, listen Aug. 22, 2017, at the sentencing hearing for Tipton in Des Moines, Iowa.
Michael Zamora/The Register

and ended up admitting that he was rigging lottery drawings and that he bought tickets around the country and asked his friends and family to do the same and involved them in claiming prizes in various states over a number of years," Neubauer said.

Tipton had left a trail along Interstate 35, which is known as a major trucking route, a drug-cartel backbone, a sex-trafficking route, and, now, the backbone of one of the biggest lottery scams ever. It's not the type of thing you'll find in the tourism happy talk on the state maps or travel guides.

Eddie Tipton was arrested on January 15, 2015 and charged with two counts of fraud. Before his trial, Robert Rhodes was also charged with two counts of fraud.

Tipton's trial began on July 13, 2015. The jury found him guilty on July 20. On September 9, Tipton was sentenced to 10 years—the maximum sentence.

Polk County District Judge Jeffrey Farrell called Tipton's actions a massive breach of trust.

Tipton's lawyer, Dean Stowers, had argued for probation because Tipton hadn't walked away with the money and was working in Texas, the Des Moines TV station KCCI reported. "He's a good person. He's honest and he's, as far as we know it, completely innocent of the charges that were filed against him and prosecuted against him in this case," Stowers said in a KCCI report.

Sand had a different view, which KCCI also reported at the time. "It is calculating decisions made one after the other according to a plan in order to attempt to defraud the Iowa Lottery," Sand said.

KCCI's Kim St. Onge asked Tipton as he left the courthouse if he had any reaction to the sentence. "Shock. That's it," the suit-wearing Tipton replied, shrugging his shoulders and smiling.

The work wasn't over.

"The sentencing is in September and we're thinking the case is over," Rich recalled. "The news media was saying it's an Iowa case, it happened in Iowa, good it will be over, and we can keep moving ahead doing good things for good causes."

thirty one
MORE CHARGES

After his conviction of two felony fraud charges in Iowa, Tipton faced more scrutiny over cases in Colorado, Kansas, Oklahoma, and Wisconsin due to Tommy Tipton's testimony about the most important hot dog purchase in lottery history.

At one point, Sand and other investigators had discovered that Rhodes and Tipton attended the University of Houston at the same time. Shortly after, they noticed on LinkedIn that they had worked together. "At that point, we knew we had them. We would need more to go on to put our case together, but we knew where to direct our efforts," Sand said.

In Eddie Tipton's interview with prosecutors after he was convicted the first time, he said he eventually saw his effort to use two lines of code to change history as something akin to "War Games" where a guy hacked in and started a nuclear war. He just wanted to see if he could hack the system but wasn't trying to blow up anything. In this case, he insists he didn't initially think of winning money.

For all his maneuvering, Tipton said he didn't have Mob ties, which prosecutors had feared at one point. He didn't have an armada of "dirty lawyers." He had given numbers to two people: his brother, and his friend, Rhodes, and that was it.

As a lottery organization employee, he knew he wasn't supposed to play the games, and he'd never won a jackpot.

"Never," he told a state agent once. "I have never won a jackpot ever in any game."

He bought lottery tickets occasionally before he started working for MUSL.

Prosecutors would eventually note that Tipton could have told Gaming Labs he had found a weakness in the software approval system, rather than use the weakness to perpetrate the biggest lottery fraud in history.

"That would have been a better action, and I wish I had done that," Tipton said in an interview with investigators.

"Honestly, probably at that point in time I was probably more concerned with getting the hard legal side of it. It didn't occur to me that I had actually broken the law by doing that." He continued to think there would be a loophole because he was just testing the system, attempting to discover if it had a weakness.

After a plea agreement, Tipton sat for another proffer session—an interview session prosecutors often use to fill in the blanks and perhaps give a criminal a chance to earn a lighter sentence.

Tipton was surprised the session was being transcribed by a court reporter. Sand told him it was to make sure he didn't lie, which would violate the plea agreement.

"Just put another noose around my neck," Tipton replied.

The conversation quickly turned to how Tipton had the idea to pull the scam. Tipton said that early in his MUSL career, accountant Gene Schaller at MUSL asked him jokingly in a hallway chat, "Hey, did you put your secret numbers in there? You can set numbers on any given day since you wrote the software."

Schaller liked to "push my buttons," Tipton noted, because while Schaller was liberal, Tipton was conservative. He, and his brother, loved guns. A felony conviction would take them away.

Tipton said he threw cold water on the idea: "No, it wouldn't work that way because it's being reviewed."

`But Tipton's mind volleyed the idea, as an I.T. professional would a more conventional software question. It was "just like a little seed that was planted," Tipton said. "And then, during one slow period, I just had a—had a thought that it's possible, and I tried it and I put it in."

He said it was just a few months after the seed was planted in the hallway.

Tipton eventually planted the code during an update that passed the single external review such machines typically got. He didn't keep a copy, so there was really no record of the change.

From then on, the language that Tipton had planted—and merely emailed to MUSL's Vegas-based contractor, Gaming Labs, or GLI, that was supposed to watch for trouble—was programmed into every machine.

"That's it," Tipton replied, like he was describing some kind of two plus two equals four equation. Simple.

"From there on it was baked into every random-number generator?" Sand asked.

"Uh huh," Eddie Tipton responded. Sand wanted to ask about "rootkits" but saved that for later. It's computer jargon. Let's just say it was more bending of reality by digital manipulation.

Gaming Labs was supposed to safeguard against any tampering. Tipton had sent the language straight to them. And the company, with all its tech knowledge, received that language for its considered review.

"What happened when you sent it over to GLI?" Sand asked.

"Nothing," Tipton deadpanned. "That was it. It was just put the software in, tried it, compiled it, and closed the software. I didn't even save it, so the change was never written anywhere." And no one had any chance of seeing it after that, Tipton noted.

thirty two
THE VIEW FROM THE INVESTIGATORS' DESKS

The case was an unusual ride for investigators.

Iowa Deputy Attorney General Thomas H. Miller came into the case in late 2011, when an anonymous person was trying to cash in the $16.5 million Hot Lotto ticket.

Miller knew at that point a fraud had occurred. Trying to cash a ticket in that way is a "low-level felony" that normally wouldn't be worth spending the kind of resources that were in play in this case, Miller said in an archival interview. "But it was a unique situation and it also was a significant and important situation because obviously the integrity of the state lottery is financially a matter of serious concern to the people of the state of Iowa."

Miller worked the case for two and half years and retired in July 2014. Considering the three-year statute of limitations, he had worked most of the heart of the investigation. But he left before the release of the video of Eddie Tipton buying the ticket—and the hot dogs seen 'round the world.

"I left before the real fun began," Miller recalled. "But we knew all along there was fraud because there were false statements in connection with an effort to cash the ticket. We didn't know until late 2014 just how extraordinary the fraud was."

Miller heard some of the armchair quarterbacking in the case.

"There has been criticism about the pace of the investigation," Miller acknowledged. "But to put it in context, we have a relatively low-level felony, even though, for the reasons I mentioned, an important one, and it might not have been entirely appropriate for the Division of Criminal Investigation to be devoting too many resources to it. In fact, they had very few resources devoted to it that weren't funded by Terry Rich's Iowa Lottery. It was his decision, and his decision entirely, to proceed with an investigation. Had he preferred to sweep the matter under the rug, so to speak, there would have been no investigation because DCI and the state are not going to fund trips out of state to try to get to the bottom of this matter."

Rich noted that funds approved for the investigation were never in question. "Our governor at the time, Terry Branstad, always said, 'I don't care about the money. Make sure the games are fair and honest.' That's Midwest ethics and leadership," Rich said.

After Johnston, the Canada lawyer, tried to cash the ticket, it was clear there was fraud, Miller recalled. Agents would need to interview him. Same with Crawford Shaw. "[Shaw] was almost completely uncooperative in efforts to interview him. Johnston was likewise extremely shy about talking to us, but the DCI agent, Matt Anderson, after a series of contacts, ultimately got an agreement for him to sit down and talk to us."

Anderson, Bogle, and Miller went to Quebec City to meet with Johnston, a native Canadian in his 70s who had spent most of his career working from an office in the Turks and Caicos islands in the Caribbean Sea. He had worked in a Toronto law firm that established tax shelters for rich Canadians, then figured out he could make more money on his own, he told Miller.

"He wanted to point out that not all of his clients were drug dealers," Miller recalled. Bogle added, "As he described how he made a living, it certainly fit the profile of somebody who was a money-launderer for drug-runners."

Johnston did business with Sonfield, who was based in Houston at an office where Crawford Shaw also worked earlier.

Johnston told Miller et al. that the people who hired him were Sonfield and his client, Robert Rhodes of Houston. Rhodes had the ticket.

"We had worked backwards from Shaw and Johnston to Rhodes and that's where we ultimately ran into a dead end because our efforts to interview Rhodes and Sonfield met with stonewalling on their part," Miller said.

"When we hit a roadblock with Sonfield and Rhodes—once all efforts to get them to cooperate were exhausted—at that point it became apparent that the only remaining source of investigation was release of the videotape. That was in spring of 2014. The case was solved in 2014, not long after I retired."

"This was a true mystery. Unraveling that was interesting and rewarding," Miller said. "Usually you have someone standing over a body with a smoking gun or you have any number of potential suspects, all of whom have a motive to commit a crime. In this case, where the fruits of the crime were $16 million, everybody on the planet has a motive to commit that crime. The question becomes how to learn who these people are that had held that ticket. It's a logical puzzle but not an easy one to solve."

The anonymity of the winner raised suspicion but could have been innocent. "Maybe they were just shy," Miller said. "But one thing we knew for sure was that when Philip Johnston talked to Mary Neubauer, he was lying" about personally buying the ticket.

thirty three
'BABY JESUS' TAKES OVER THE CASE

It would have been easy to underestimate Sand, Porter would later recall. Here was a baby-faced lawyer who looked like a young assistant handling a case until the "real lawyer" showed up. Porter couldn't get over how much Sand looked like Jace Norman, the teenage star of the Nickelodeon superhero series, "Henry Danger."

Sand was so serious his extended family called him "Baby Jesus," among other names he didn't use on business cards.

That kind of street cred—the kind that comes with any comparison to the great "I Am"—would certainly have helped Sand in this situation. He was replacing Miller, a senior prosecutor who drew respect and fear— even from the defense lawyers who were assigned to try to fend off his tough prosecutions. Miller was the most experienced criminal prosecutor in the state. Sand, by comparison, and by looks, was a kid.

"But Sand knew what he was doing," Porter recalled. He was Iowa's go-to guy—really its only guy—going after financial crimes. He often beat more experienced lawyers in cases.

So it fell to Sand to expand the slim accordion file Miller had handed him—to build a case against Eddie Tipton, piece by piece, fact by fact. To close in on the truth.

Some members of the public mistakenly thought Tipton was dumb. There is a difference, Sand said, between being dumb and making mistakes.

"People put too much stock in either intelligence or stupidity as a static factor in someone's life," Sand said. "I can wake up in the morning and have a certain level of intelligence and do something really stupid because I'm not thinking about it, or I'm tired, or because I'm stressed. Everyone makes mistakes. That's how we catch people, through their mistakes.

"If Eddie had come up with a better alibi, if Eddie had not purchased that ticket himself, there are a couple of steps along the way that would have changed the outcome of this case. If his brother had not tried to launder the winnings of that Colorado ticket to the point the FBI started snooping around…it again would have been very difficult to put together this case.

"We're talking about, over the course of 2004 to 2014, a handful of mistakes in 10 years. We had to work very hard to find the right mistakes in that time frame to put this case together. No one is immune from making them," Sand added.

That meant spending more time with agents than with his wife, Sand said. Days ran to midnight sometimes.

"We had a good team that was focused on getting down to the bottom of it. No naysayers. If Terry Rich had said, 'Look, you guys have a couple of tickets, I don't want to contribute or assist anymore, and I want this all to be over with,' [things would have been tougher]," Sand said. But Rich and the rest of the team were all in.

Their talk of what to nickname the case expanded from the "I-35 Lottery Case" to "The Eddie Tipton Friends and Family Plan."

"I didn't have a shorthand, but I know the folks at the Iowa Lottery were calling it the Eddie Tipton Friends and Family Plan. I thought it was a pretty good fit," Sand said.

There were 600 court filings in the two trials of Eddie Tipton. Those were in addition to everyone's regular workload. "Those were a very busy three years," Sand said.

It was grueling work that, in the end, succeeded.

But Sand wasn't without his own difficult periods during the case. After the birth of his second son, he had a deposition scheduled, with the agreement he would move them if necessary. But the defense attorney wanted to argue about the delay. Sand ended up having intense discussions with the judge and the defense attorney over the first few days of his new son's life. "That was definitely the low point," Sand recalled.

High points? "It's not just one mountain. It's a whole range, and it's hard to pick out which is the tallest."

Getting the case finished was one high peak. So was finding the seven tickets that looked fishy.

Sand had offered a plea agreement on the Iowa ticket, and it was refused.

Rhodes' attorney told Sand he didn't think the state had much against Tipton.

thirty four
RHODES FEARS DOUBLE TROUBLE

A turning point in the case had been Rhodes' decision in December 2015 to take a plea deal that included helping prosecutors make the case.

Porter said Rhodes signed a proffer agreement with Iowa prosecutors but he had to finesse how to handle the Wisconsin jackpot situation.

"Ultimately, the weight of the evidence caused Robert Rhodes to decide it was in his interest to cooperate with authorities," Porter said. "He ultimately did."

"He entered into a proffer agreement [with Iowa]," Porter said. "It took some time to arrange because Robert Rhodes was not only of interest to Iowa authorities. Wisconsin authorities had some interest in him too. So he didn't want to cooperate with us and then become entangled with authorities in Wisconsin without a similar deal.

At one point, Rhodes decided to testify against Eddie Tipton in the initial case. And as that progressed, the broader case came into view. That piled charges on Eddie Tipton, who already had been convicted of fraud and had appealed.

"Ultimately we came to a compromise. He provided information to law enforcement that was helpful and corroborated largely what our forensic analysts had already obtained with respect to how the machine worked. He also identified that he was involved in the claiming of the

Wisconsin jackpot, that he had a role in receiving and passing along the Hot Lotto ticket in Iowa, and that he was willing to testify against Eddie Tipton on those grounds," Porter said.

"From there, the two individuals left were Eddie Tipton and Tommy Tipton. Both, I think, realized that they were facing legal jeopardy in multiple states. Iowa had an active prosecution of ongoing criminal conduct with the possibility of 20 to 30 years of prison per defendant," Porter said.

"But with respect to Tommy, and with respect to Eddie, Kansas had concerns about 2by2. Colorado and Oklahoma had concerns with Tommy with respect to the jackpot claims there. They saw that they had some real obstacles to retaining their freedom, and they decided it was better for them to cut a deal. Ultimately, they did," Porter said.

At a news conference announcing that the jackpots in Colorado and Wisconsin had been tied to Eddie Tipton and had brought additional felony charges, Jim Saunders, director of investigative operations for the Iowa Department of Public Safety, noted the case had gone national. He asked people who knew of someone claiming a prize for someone else to visit a Survey Monkey site.

"This investigation demonstrates the Department of Public Safety, the lottery and the attorney general's commitment to ensuring that the lottery's games are of the utmost integrity. This is a very active, ongoing investigation," Saunders said.

At the same news conference, Rich noted he was president of a national lottery association. He said the nation's lotteries would work together to solve the cases.

"Now, some people have questioned why we stuck with this case so long," Rich said. "Well, the answer is simple: That's our job. It's our responsibility as lotteries to offer games and prizes with systems and procedures built upon fairness and integrity. These charges stem from the actions of those who apparently were willing to risk the consequences of committing fraud in an attempt to secure a lottery prize.

"It's appalling to know that the person at the center of this case once worked at a vendor organization within the lottery industry," Rich continued. "This is a breach of trust against lotteries, our players, our games, and the billions of dollars at stake for the worthy causes that lotteries benefit."

Rich said the case helped lotteries improve security and showed that lotteries and other businesses must continue to guard against fraud.

Saunders said the case was different than any case he'd seen in 30 years in law enforcement. But Rich said, like any other case, this one brought immediate security changes, including additional safeguards designed to ensure that no one person had "all the keys to the kingdom."

"Based on our investigation," said Porter, "we identified a Colorado state jackpot in 2005, a Wisconsin state jackpot in 2007, the attempted claim of a Hot Lotto jackpot in Iowa in 2010, a claim of two Kansas 2by2 jackpots in 2010, and a Hot Lotto jackpot from Oklahoma in 2011 that were, in one way or another, tied back to Eddie Tipton."

thirty five
THE END GAME

With delays, Eddie Tipton's case spilled into 2016. Rich took lottery players questions live online in January, nearly a month before a lawsuit was filed by people who claimed they were cheated by what looked like a rigging of a drawing on a date for which they had bought tickets. Tommy Tipton was charged soon after.

After receiving documents in a freedom of information request, the Associated Press reported that Strutt, who had guided MUSL since it began 28 years earlier, was ousted in late 2015. He was paid $284,000 in severance, the Associated Press reported.

Eventually, the Iowa Supreme Court threw out Tipton's conviction for tampering with equipment, arguing that the state hadn't adequately explained why it took more than the three years allowed to bring charges. But the court held that the state's contention was valid that the statute of limitations clock on the fraud charge related to trying to cash the ticket should have started with Shaw and McLean's efforts on January 17, 2012. In effect, the court ordered a new trial on that charge, Porter said.

In its decision, the court noted that Justice Brent Appel faulted investigators for taking too long to try to interview key witnesses in Canada and Texas. Appel thought the state lacked due diligence and didn't deserve an extension on the statute of limitations—and could have

Mug Shots: Eddie Tipton, Robert Rhodes, and Tommy Tipton

stayed within the legal limitations. Division of Criminal Investigation agent Matt Anderson testified that his efforts were delayed by a busy workload, which included dozens of voter fraud cases.

But it was all moot because Tipton had already made a plea deal on the broader case.

Eddie Tipton, the man who thought he could beat the system, threw down his cards—or perhaps his random-number generator—and pleaded guilty in a deal. His brother, who faced at least a short time without the prospect of finding Bigfoot, unless Bigfoot had been incarcerated in Edwards County, Texas, did the same.

In June 2017, Eddie Tipton, after two years of denials, pleaded guilty to new charges, admitting he played a central role in the biggest lottery scam in U.S. history. He told the judge he couldn't remember when he first wrote the code that changed everything, but he agreed that it was 2005 or 2006. "It was more of a 'trying to see if I could do it' scenario," the Des Moines Register reported. "And then it just continued to exist...the opportunity was there, and I took advantage of it."

Because the states accepted the code he wrote, Eddie Tipton considered it a "loophole" and not breaking the law, he told the court.

"I wrote software that included code that allowed me to technically predict winning numbers and I gave those numbers to other individuals who then won the lottery and shared those winnings with me," he said. "I didn't think that anybody was breaking the law at all by giving numbers away. But I gave the numbers away knowing that someone could win," the Register quoted Tipton.

Both Eddie and Tommy got jail time. Eddie's sentence was left up to a judge. Tommy got a much shorter sentence.

"Both agreed to cooperate with authorities, which was useful to us so that we could try and make sure that all of our questions were answered. We want to make sure that we learn everything possible from this, so the industry as a whole is better positioned to defend against fraud in the future," Porter said.

The plea deal called for Eddie Tipton, then 54, to serve up to 25 years, but the thought was he would probably be out in few years with good behavior. The maximum with credit for good behavior would be 10 years.

The Tipton brothers also agreed to pay $2.2 million in restitution to the Colorado, Kansas, Oklahoma, and Wisconsin lotteries.

Eddie had scammed lotteries in Colorado, Kansas, Wisconsin, and Oklahoma. He had tried to cheat Iowa but failed.

Iowa turned out to be the only state Tipton and his team tried to scam that didn't pay a prize. Hot Lotto was retired by the states in October 2017.

Tipton stood before Polk County (Iowa) District Judge Brad McCall for sentencing. He was apologetic.

"I certainly regret" what happened, Tipton said at the sentencing hearing. "It's difficult even saying that with all the people I know behind me that I hurt, and I regret it. I'm sorry."

McCall said he could tell Tipton was intelligent. He told him to spend time in prison thinking about what he had done.

"It is indeed unfortunate that you did not use that intelligence to prosper by legal means," McCall said. "Instead you chose an illegal path."

Lottery officials got their say in front of the TV cameras after court adjourned.

"We're glad that the court agreed and found it appropriate to send Mr. Tipton to prison," Sand said.

In a prepared statement, Rich said:

"This moment has been years coming and provides closure and certainty after all this time.

"Every organization will face tests throughout its history, and this case certainly was one for our lottery. It's disconcerting that someone who worked at a vendor organization within the lottery industry chose to betray the trust placed in him for his own personal gain. We're glad that the judicial system worked and that this case has been solved.

"This case is an important reminder to lotteries everywhere to keep monitoring and making improvements to stay ahead of those who would try to beat the system. It was the security procedures at our lottery that caught this fraud attempt and prevented a multi-million-dollar jackpot from being paid out.

"We're proud of the work done in this case and thank the Iowa Attorney General's Office and the Iowa Division of Criminal Investigation for their dedication and professionalism in achieving this outcome.

"Some might say this case represented our lottery's worst day, but in retrospect, I also believe it was our best day in terms of the information we learned and the enhanced procedures and processes we have in place today to protect against the vulnerabilities identified. We thank our players for their understanding through this long-running case as the process ensured that justice was served.

"I have absolute confidence in the integrity of Iowa Lottery's games today and know that they offer everyone the same fair shot at winning."

Tommy Tipton pleaded guilty to a felony charge of conspiracy to commit theft and a misdemeanor theft charge. As part of the deal, Iowa dropped the felony charge of ongoing criminal conduct. Tommy agreed to pay more than $800,000 and was sentenced to 75 days in jail.

Eddie Tipton is put in handcuffs Tuesday, Aug. 22, 2017, after being sentenced to 25 years for his role in a lottery scam at the Polk County Courthouse in Des Moines. Michael Zamora/The Register

By then, the Tipton brothers were both living in Flatonia, Texas. Eddie had pleaded guilty in Wisconsin to fraud and computer crime for a 2007 lottery case in that state involving a $783,000 Megabucks jackpot. He faced up to five and a half years in prison for the Wisconsin case, but that was to be served at the same time as the Iowa term—not on top of it.

For his central role in the overall case, Eddie Tipton pleaded guilty to three felony charges in Iowa and Wisconsin of ongoing criminal conduct, theft by fraud, and computer crime. Prosecutors said Tipton conspired with friends and family in claiming lottery prizes in Colorado, Kansas, Oklahoma, and Wisconsin and attempting to claim the lottery jackpot in Iowa. He received up to 25 years in prison on this round of charges and currently is serving time in a Clarinda, Iowa prison.

Eddie Tipton, who turned 55 on March 15, 2018, is prisoner number 6832975. He gets up at 6:15 a.m. for breakfast, cleans his room, then has a couple of hours to use the yard, library, gym, or work. Lunch is at 11. After cleanup, Tipton has the same open time as he does in the morning.

Dinner is at 4, then cleanup. Then another round of free time runs until 9, and the guards count prisoners for the third time that day. Tipton can visit the dayroom from 9:30 to 11 p.m., then it's back to the cell for the night.

Tipton has been in prison since August 25, 2017. His case will be reviewed in July 2019, and the parole board could decide to set a date for his release or order him to serve more of his sentence.

Tommy Tipton pleaded guilty in the case to a felony and a misdemeanor charge of conspiracy to commit theft. Rhodes, of Sugar Land, Texas, pleaded guilty to a felony charge of being party to a computer crime.

A plea agreement called for Rhodes to serve six months' home confinement in Texas and pay $409,000 in restitution to the state of Wisconsin. Tommy Tipton was sentenced in June to 75 days in jail.

After the sentencing, Sand stood with Rich to talk to reporters at the Polk County Courthouse. Sand, in a dark suit, white shirt, and blue tie, said something appropriate: "When you are an insider who abuses your position of trust and privilege you should expect to see the inside of a jail cell."

A reporter asked if Sand thought the state would recover a "significant" amount of money. Sand noted both Tipton brothers and Robert Rhodes had "significant assets." Ironically, even though Iowa state investigators spent the most time working this case, Iowa wasn't granted restitution— from the defendants or from MUSL—because the Iowa Lottery didn't pay the Hot Lotto prize at issue.

Sand was asked if justice would be served if Eddie Tipton, the ringleader in the biggest lottery scam in American history, walked in three to five years. "In this case, it's hard to say exactly what justice is when you have something so unprecedented," Sand said. "There's not much to compare it to. I think that he is agreeing to repay everything that he owes and he answered every question that we were interested in asking—and there were a lot over six hours. The fact that he is going to serve years in prison is appropriate."

Sand also told a reporter that it was a lottery employee in Maine who set prosecutors on Tipton's trail. "It all comes back to Michael Boardman from the Maine Lottery submitting through Survey Monkey a tip that he thinks that man in the video buying the ticket is Eddie Tipton. When we received that tip, along with many, many others, [Tipton] automatically became more interesting because of his place of employment on MUSL, and he had a reason not to be identified as having purchased that ticket. As soon has his name came in to me, he was absolutely a suspect."

Reporters asked Rich what the sentencing meant to him. "This is a big day for the Iowa Lottery and, I think, lotteries across America because it brings certainty and clarity to one of the most, I think, strange and unique lottery cases in history."

"This was an emotional feeling. It was a violation of trust," Rich said. "We're relieved and we're grateful" that the team of prosecutors and investigators amassed enough evidence to bring a guilty plea, he added. He was happy that his first big legal case ended with an admission of guilt by Tipton, which was a clear win for the state.

A reporter asked whether the lottery's image had been soiled by the scam. "Any time you talk about someone on the inside doing fraud, you have concern," Rich said. "On the other hand, I think our players stuck with us because they saw we weren't going to give up." Investigators discovered what had happened so it could be addressed, Rich said.

"We're never perfect. Just like my computer at home; I'm always getting a new patch, and updates to the patches, and then tomorrow someone will try to break in, and I'll have to get a new patch. We're doing the same thing the lottery industry is. We are looking and trying to stay one step ahead of anyone who might try to do something illegal."

Sand said the suggestion that the Iowa Lottery might have gotten a public relations black eye out of the case showed the reporter "didn't know the details."

"The only reason any of this happened today is because the Iowa Lottery said, 'We're not going to pay this ticket here in Iowa until we are assured that the people who purchased it and everyone who possessed it is not a prohibited player in any way and was acting legally and appropriately," Sand said. "That's the only reason any of this came to light. They could have paid it out and we could have had no idea and it could still be going on today. It was the Iowa Lottery that said, under threat of lawsuit, the Iowa Lottery stuck to its guns and said, 'No, we're not paying it out.' The criminal investigation began because of that.

"What it comes down to is we kept at it, we kept working, we didn't get discouraged when we hit roadblocks, and we're at the end of the day, and we got our man," Sand said as Rich smiled and nodded at his side.

Someone asked about whether lottery sales had suffered.

"Our sales have continued to grow and be record-breaking across the board. Part of that is the transparency. Our staff said what we think happened. Let's work and tell the public to be vigilant when you get tickets. Sign your tickets. Check your tickets," Rich said.

thirty six
LESSONS LEARNED

The whole thing took the wind out of lottery colleagues who had trusted Eddie Tipton.

"Crimes against trust to me are in ways more problematic than others," Sand said.

"We all know that there are people out there who might be willing to push us down or hit us over the head or wave a gun in our face and take what we have," Sand said. "But when they do that, it's hard for us to conceive of that as something that we did wrong. We might think, 'Well, I should have been walking somewhere else or I should have gone inside when I saw that person following me. But it's very different when it's someone you know, you have worked with, you have trusted for years on end who abuses that trust. The questions that can remain with a person about their ability to judge another person's character or their own ability to assess whether someone is a good person or not remain with that person who is a victim who has had their trust violated for a much longer time. They are much deeper wounds."

Coppess took his job as vice president of security right after Tipton was convicted of the initial charges. He recalled Rich telling him they were going to make sure it didn't happen again.

Coppess sought to lower expectations. "I was a little forward, probably, but I cautioned him, 'Let's not say we're not going to let it happen, but we're going to set up processes so that if it does happen we're going to catch it sooner than later.'

"That was based on my experience with a person in our property room [at the West Des Moines police department] stealing from us—taking something from right under our nose—and how that makes you feel internally. Here is this person who was close to us. We were friends, and they took from us. I suspected that was a similar feeling that was going on inside the Iowa Lottery."

Then there is the trouble with the credibility of lotteries—though sales of Iowa tickets rose after this scandal.

"The other problem is that we get into a situation where the trust in institutions begins to decline. Where you have people involved in institutions, like the lottery system, who abuse their status, who abuse their privilege as insiders, people start to think, 'Well, what can I trust in this world?' We have to have a system where we can rely upon institutions, because that is how our society functions, how our government functions. In that sense, those crimes against trust by insiders can be much more damaging in the long run.

"It's a textbook lesson in what could happen to someone in public life and how to handle that. I guess history will tell if we handled it correctly."

CBS had called the Eddie Tipton scam one of the largest in the United States and maybe the world.

"A lot of people said, 'Why is this such a big deal? There are murders and all kinds of things that affect people's lives. Why would the lottery be that important?'" Rich said.

"Most people don't realize that the lottery sells $80 billion in tickets in the United States each year. That's more than the NFL, Major League Baseball, the NBA, the music industry, and the movie industry combined. It's almost $20 billion in monies for good causes. My counterparts often said, 'If you screw this up, that's going to cost a lot of people and a lot of good causes a lot of money.' It really had a lot of pressure to make sure we handled it right.

"From the beginning, our team completely said we will do whatever it takes to find out what happened and to solve this. And all our bosses—the governors, the legislators and the state of Iowa—continue to say, 'Do what it takes. We don't care about the money. We care about the fairness and the honesty of the Iowa Lottery.'

"If we didn't keep the integrity of the Lottery intact, we would have lost a lot more.

"This isn't the first time that there was fraud in the lottery industry," with its hundreds of millions of normally routine transactions, Rich said. "There were five incidents worldwide in lotteries that occurred going back to 1980. The first was in 1980 in Pennsylvania. It was called the 6-6-6 Caper, where some employees, insiders, put latex paint inside ping pong balls to determine the winner. The case was featured in the John Travolta movie 'Lucky Numbers.'

"Another one happened in Pennsylvania that instead of balls used a random-number generator. The person's name was Arthur Henry Rich. My last name is Rich, what a coincidence, huh? He was a jockey but also a computer programmer. He created a ticket after a drawing to claim a $15 million prize.

"In the 1990s, a guy named Ron Harris in Nevada—he was on the Nevada Gaming Commission—figured out a way with the random-number generators that were in slot machines to be able to predict when a jackpot would come up. He was busted. There's one going on now where they think Russian hackers are going after a certain vendor of slot machines' random-number generators to try to predict when numbers are going to appear."

Porter said it was important for the state to get Eddie Tipton's take on how this all went down, again, because in some ways the fate of an $80 billion U.S. industry hung in the balance.

"We have testimony from [Eddie Tipton] about what he did and why he did it," Porter said. "You don't always have that opportunity. Defendants aren't required to testify against themselves. They have constitutional protection against that. So when you get a jury verdict, as we did in the first case, it can feel kind of hollow. We knew we had the right defendant in the first case. We knew we had the right crime in the first case. I think there were always lingering concerns that we didn't necessarily have the right theory. The prosecution had moved forward in the theory regarding a rootkit. MUSL logs showed that on November 20, 2010, about a month before the disputed draw, Eddie Tipton had access to the MUSL [random-number generator] machine, purportedly to change the time.

"The prosecution's theory at the time was Eddie Tipton put malicious code on the machine at that time that allowed him to anticipate what the outcome of the draw was going to be. I think since we've learned that the reality was a bit subtler. The malicious code was probably on those machines from the moment they were built, but Eddie Tipton's malicious code triggered from a variety of criteria and one of those was time of draw. If the clock wasn't right, the malicious code would not have worked right.

"There is certainly satisfaction from that point. We have a better handle on what occurred. We spent a lot of time internally trying to brainstorm—how could this have occurred? Could someone have used magnets? Could somebody have shut off the random-number generator before the numbers were drawn? Could someone have somehow manipulated the seed in the random-number generator? Could it have been put on after the fact with the rootkit?

"We obviously have to protect against all of those potential risks, and we do, every day. But this was a useful exercise in that we were able to ascertain how he did it, confirm how he did it, and we're protecting against that today."

Jobes remembers thinking how odd the case was when he got briefed on the details after he took his job at the Iowa Division of Criminal Investigation. "All those pieces from Texas to Canada to New York and the offshore investment account," he recalled, pausing to shake his head. "This is just crazy stuff for a ticket in Iowa. It was really amazing to me, the effort that our defendants went to try to make this thing work."

He chuckled over Bigfoot's appearance in the case file.

"I didn't know what to make of that, to be honest," Jobes said. "It was just an interesting side story to one of the defendants. Wow, we're chasing Bigfoot and that's how we're getting people to help us out. It was a good laugh."

For Miller, the Iowa deputy attorney general, the discovery that Tipton had altered the system was a huge surprise.

Fraud Key Elements

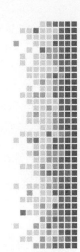

Source: Association of Certified Fraud Examiners

"I was flabbergasted" that Eddie Tipton was the architect of the fraud, Miller said. "We had kind of discounted the prospect that someone was manipulating the lottery. I was shocked and amazed that the person who was the beneficial owner of that ticket had actually manipulated the computer generation of the winning number. This is extraordinary. Most of us would believe there is no way a lottery could be manipulated. It's surprising to learn that that is not the case."

The case showed that things made by humans are "fallible," Miller said.

But there also were high points. "The case was fun, interesting, and different," Miller said. "An interesting white collar crime that was, in effect, a mystery was fun to work on." He spent most of his career solving murders.

"I was gratified to see that this case reached a very full and satisfying conclusion from the standpoint of not only correcting a bad actor but also in improving a system and also in justifying the trust and faith that the head of the Iowa Lottery put in all of us to try to get to the bottom of this."

thirty seven
A MATTER OF TRUST

For Sand and others, the case was not only a lesson on greed, but also a matter of trust.

"It comes down to trust," Sand said. "We have to have trust in each other. But you have to at the same time recognize that if you rely on trust alone you are giving people an opportunity and also a temptation to take advantage of their position. I remember growing up in a small town in Iowa and my dad would always lock the car doors. I remember asking him why. It's not like there is any crime here in Decorah. And he would say, 'Well we don't want to tempt people.' That stuck with me the rest of my life. It makes sense."

Eddie Tipton had been tempted by those computers, those codes, and the prizes to which they led.

thirty eight
WHY DIDN'T ANYONE SEE THIS COMING?

MUSL has been decidedly tight-lipped about this whole affair, but the questions remained over how this fraud wasn't caught sooner and why Eddie Tipton was hired despite at least a minor rap sheet.

Jobes took the broad view. "You know you can work very diligently to screen your employees, to monitor your employees, and do background work. At the end of all of that, ultimately, they are going to make a decision about how they are going to behave going forward. You can look at past behavior, and it may be an indicator, but really you are putting some faith in those employees that they are going to conduct themselves in the way that you expect them to in the course of their duties. In this case, that turned out to not be true, with Mr. Tipton taking advantage of his position."

Coppess noted the case was complicated by having several states involved. "Getting people to buy in to the idea that a fraud was committed was an uphill battle. And going to these other states that might have had a fraud and getting them to have the same values that you already expect was an uphill battle to this case." Even getting different branches of law enforcement to work together was a challenge, Coppess noted. "They don't have the same interest in your case. This was a task force and everyone should have been working together, but I don't know that we ever achieved that. Iowa overcame that by working with its own resources. In any big case, multijurisdictional, be it bank robbers or something, it needs that overseeing governance or supervision to say, 'We are in different places, but we are having the same thing happen to us, so I am now in charge. I am the overseer.' Then everybody else needs to fall under them. That was a really big battle for this particular case to get that to finally happen."

Bogle was surprised other authorities were slow to jump on the case or never did.

"To me, I believe the entire industry should have been on board with this because it attacked the integrity of our games," Bogle said. "I was surprised somewhat by the reluctance of some of the other representatives or other state lotteries to aggressively pursue this. I wanted to know how this happened so we could make sure it didn't happen again. There are 44 state lotteries and each one of those states relies on some of that funding for the programs that they support.

"I just felt it was important to solve this to figure out what happened, why it happened and not let it happen again. This was huge. What if we had paid this and found out later [it was fraud?] The money would have been gone. It's a great case study of insider threat. Technology is wonderful, but this could have all been avoided, I believe, if there had been proper oversight and if there had been proper segregation of duties.

"It's not a technical solution. It's a human solution. Eddie had all the keys to the castle. You can't let that happen. That's not just at lotteries with [random-number generators]. We deal with that in all kinds of industries across this nation as we get into the cyber world. There has to be proper oversight and governance and there has to be segregation of duties so that you mitigate the opportunities for this kind of activity."

Bogle was glad the Iowa team stuck to its legal stand on how lottery tickets need to be cashed, in their interpretation.

"I was really proud of the senior leadership of the Iowa Lottery through that. Big games and big prizes create churn, which creates more money for state programs. I understand that. It had to be difficult. I know there was external pressure to pay. We had a great team here that stood their ground and believed that integrity was of the utmost importance and backed by a governor who said, 'Look, I want you to make money, but more important to me is the integrity of the game,'" Bogle said.

There were concerns of blowing it and facing a house-cleaning at the lottery. There were concerns of lawsuits against the lottery. There was the risk of paying a prize that was ill-gotten. The Iowa Lottery stuck to its guns. There was no payment.

The Iowa team's work was complicated by an industry lack of cooperation from many states when prosecutors went looking for patterns among jackpot wins, Porter said. In fact, there were some who wanted to bring Sand—who won election to become state auditor beginning in January 2019—on sanctions for "prosecutorial misconduct."

"Once Rob Sand had the tip about Tommy Tipton winning the jackpot, Sand wanted to get data from across the country on lottery wins," Porter recalled. "He and I worked closely in September and October 2015 to figure out a way to do it.

"Sand knew what he needed to find to prove up his criminal claims. I knew how to contact the rest of the state lotteries. I also had some thoughts on the sorts of sales and game data that lotteries would have in their systems. I talked Sand into lowering the dollar threshold on the search to $10,000, arguing that unless he was sure he was just fishing for whales the number needed to be lower. We ultimately agreed this dollar value was low enough to make the search feasible but high enough to make it worthwhile.

"I emailed every U.S. lottery state in October 2015, asking for lotteries to provide the following information for all winners of $10,000 and above from 2003 to the present, for lottery games where winning numbers were selected via RNG."

They asked for:
— Winner Name
— Winner City and State
— Draw Date
— Prize Claim Date (between January 1, 2003 and the present)
— Prize Amount ($10,000 or above)

— Game Name

— Quick Pick vs. Manual play, if that information can be readily ascertained within your records and system.

"Some states were extremely helpful and responsive, like Kentucky, Wisconsin, and Colorado," Porter said. But there were others that were offended.

"Others were not happy at all. One lottery's lawyer threatened sanctions, and I ultimately had to intervene and smooth things over," Porter said.

Porter defended the approach: "My view: Sand was always acting properly and ethically. He was just following the evidence where it led."

thirty nine
GREED AND AMBITION, OR MAYBE JUST GREED

In the Shakespeare play, Macbeth realized that greed and ambition were all that were motivating him to kill and replace the king, but he continues with the plan.

> "I HAVE NO SPUR TO PRICK THE SIDES OF MY INTENT, BUT ONLY VAULTING AMBITION, WHICH O'ER LEAPS ITSELF AND FALLS ON THE OTHER."
> —SHAKESPEARE'S MACBETH

Eddie Tipton had hot dogs. And they weren't going to pierce his ambition. But they were enough to help him fall on the ambition of others.

"There will always be someone trying to beat the system; that's the bottom line," Rich said. "As the regulators—as the overseers—the importance of having good regulations and oversight proves true even with the Eddie Tipton case that we want to be able to keep the games fair and honest at all times.

"I've heard a lot of people talk about how complicated this case was, like finding a needle in a haystack. What I would classify it as is trying to find a needle in a haystack, but you didn't know which haystack to look in."

When asked what he would tell Eddie Tipton if he had the chance, the DCI assistant director, Jobes, said: "You got greedy and you got caught."

Jobes noted there is no perfect system. "The best you can do is to put good technological barriers in place, put good controls in place, multiple levels of approval for key functions, having proper oversight over those key functions. And being very diligent in those individuals that you hire and monitoring those employees. That really is the best you can do."

Some thought the whole case took too long.

Miller, the man who pitched the case to Sand on his way to retirement, said much of the trouble came because of lack of resources.

The Iowa Division of Criminal Investigation was forced by tight budgets to prioritize—to focus on the felonies of murders, rapes, and kidnappings, Miller said.

The Tipton case was a step down on the prosecutorial ladder—a Class B felony case. "It was a unique case and an important case that nevertheless struggled for investigators' hours," Miller said in an interview. "Resources in Iowa state government during that time—and during most of the time I have been practicing law in the state—are limited, and it was not a case that could receive priority that one gives a high-profile murder case.

"In a murder case, one is concerned about the public safety if someone is at large with a knife or gun. There is an immediate concern about somebody else being harmed, whereas this case was not a case in which there was a significant or really any public safety issue presently at stake that required urgency."

The Iowa prosecutors carried on. "If we hadn't continued to be able to find the computers all across the U.S.—17 states, nearly 50 computers— and encouraged people to change them out, in my opinion, it would still be happening today," Rich said.

Computer scientists from Iowa State University and the University of Iowa, former FBI and CIA agents, and others helped to crack the case. Rich called famed lawyer and politician Rudy Giuliani and asked how he kept going during a famous junk-bond case. "You have to," Giuliani replied.

Rich would later develop a keynote with tips for other regulators that included the following:

— Internal fraud is as much of a threat as external fraud.
— Trust, but verify.
— Your business, jobs, and friendships could be at risk.
— Keep your eyes open for the key elements of fraud.

As Rich thought about Tipton, he noted that the most notorious criminal in lottery history exhibited at least four behavioral red flags identified by the Association of Certified Fraud Examiners in its 10th biennial "Report to the Nations" regarding fraud on the job:

— He complained about inadequate pay
— Excessive pressure from within the organization
— Social isolation
— Past legal problems
— Living beyond one's means and financial difficulties.

Coppess said criminals in cases like this are done in by arrogance. "It is the belief that they are smarter than anybody else. For a criminal investigator such as myself, we like people like that because at some point they want to tell you about everything they did. They kind of want to get caught, because in their head, they never get credit for how smart they are until they tell the world. In interviews, you really want to let that person know you are interested in hearing about how smart they are and how they beat all of us. It is that arrogance and the need to get attention that probably created the biggest missteps and ultimately the discovery of Mr. Tipton's malicious acts. I'm really thankful that occurred."

Coppess said a case like Tipton's takes a toll on the victims of the fraud, including the lottery personnel charged with protecting the integrity of their slice of the $80 billion U.S. lottery industry.

Those who are burned by fraud feel "emotions of anger and loss," Coppess said. "This person—you trusted him. When someone cheats you, it makes you feel stupid, embarrassed. We go to this place of, 'How does that make me look?' Then, 'I want this person to pay.' Recognizing you feel that way is part of the recovery.

"Hopefully, going forward, some of the feelings that we have and the work we do is taking the lesson we've learned from Eddie Tipton and what he was able to do to commit a fraud, put processes in place, but also work to make him not be so important," Coppess said. "For some people's belief system, it's even going so far as forgiving him. I don't know that people will get to that. But I think for us to carry him less in our head and not focus so much on Eddie Tipton will be better for us as individuals and ultimately pay dividends for us, the Iowa Lottery. Everybody is on a different level on that and their timeline for recovery is set by them."

The case also caused more than a few to wonder if lotteries were clean and safe to play. They are, insist Rich, Coppess, and others.

"It is safe to play," Coppess said. "The risk of getting cheated is about as small as it could be. As I came into the Iowa Lottery, I was impressed by this huge information system that allows us to track all of our product, to track all of our plays. Now, we aren't trying to look into the lives of our players, but if there is a call to us about something bad that happened, we have a great system to look into what happened. We educate players. We tell them if they sign the ticket (and you should), it helps establish ownership. We want to prove that a product was legally purchased, legally possessed, and then legally presented. We want people to sign a ticket as soon as they get it."

For Rich, the case was a mental puzzle that was taxing and perhaps felt like cerebral abuse.

"Being a victim is an interesting thing," Rich said. "I've never been the victim of a violent crime. This was more being a victim of a mental crime. And it's awful. You can't talk about the crime. We had a gag order for a long time on what we could and couldn't say, yet you wanted to scream to the high heavens that this happened and we know how it happened.

"Many people didn't want to do anything until it was absolute so that Eddie couldn't come back and sue over a false accusation. So we let the justice systems go on, but the mental piece of this is probably the hardest when it's all said and done.

"But closure is phenomenal. The idea that the evidence was so solid that ultimately he admitted it and pleaded guilty, as did [Tommy Tipton and Robert Rhodes], that we got the cases wrapped up with one ribbon was a much better outcome."

For Neubauer, the lottery communications exec whose suspicions had been raised by that telephone call from a Canadian lawyer detailed at the beginning of this book, it became clear that the public was confused about the fact that Eddie Tipton worked for MUSL and not the Iowa Lottery. That fact is a large reason the case took longer to solve, she noted.

Neubauer, too, has heard concerns over lottery security, but in her view, it's about managing risks.

"Some members of the public want us to say that absolutely our system is perfect, it's infallible, it can never be compromised again," Neubauer said. "I just tell them, 'Look, as long as human beings are involved in anything, that process or that procedure will never be perfect. You just need to have the best safeguards and the best systems and procedures in place that you can so that if something does start to go wrong, you can recognize that quickly, catch it, and then put even better safeguards in place as you move ahead.'"

Because, though it's unlikely, you never know when someone will somehow stir together computer fraud, bogus lotto tickets, Bigfoot, and hot dogs from a convenience store and make an $80 billion gamble that threatens an entire industry. In this case, the investigators and prosecutors won.

TIMELINE

December 23, 2010
A $10 Hot Lotto ticket is purchased at a Des Moines convenience store with two plays for five consecutive drawings.

December 29, 2010
One of the plays on that ticket matches all six numbers selected in that night's Hot Lotto drawing to win the jackpot ($16.5 million annuity, $10.8 million cash option).

Throughout 2011
The Iowa Lottery issues reminders that the winning ticket is still unclaimed and the deadline to claim the prize is 4 p.m. December 29, 2011.

December 29, 2011
The winning ticket is presented at lottery headquarters in Des Moines less than two hours before the deadline. No member of Hexham Investments Trust, the entity claiming the prize, is present. The two lawyers from the Davis Brown law firm in Des Moines who presented the ticket said they couldn't say who purchased the ticket, where it had been for the past year, and who the prize winner(s) were. The lottery continued to seek information.

January 17, 2012
Crawford Shaw, the trustee who signed the winning ticket on behalf of the trust, meets with lottery officials. He states that he misspelled the name of the trust, which was properly named Hexham Investments Trust. While some documents relating to the trust are presented, they do not provide the details sought by the lottery—notably, the name of the person who bought the ticket. Shaw said he is not the winner and did not purchase the winning ticket. He also stated he did not know the information sought by the lottery, but that the trust is based in Belize.

January 23, 2012

After 13 months of hoping to pay the prize to a legitimate winner, the Iowa Lottery sets a deadline of 3 p.m. January 27, 2012, for the requested information to be provided. If it wasn't, the lottery noted, the jackpot claim would be denied.

January 25, 2012

The trust makes an offer to the lottery, stating that if the lottery will pay the prize, the entire prize winnings will be given to charity. However, the required information sought by the lottery is not provided.

January 26, 2012

The lottery denies the offer and continues to seek the information it has requested. At 6:05 p.m., the lottery receives confirmation that the jackpot claim has been withdrawn. At 7 p.m., the lottery holds a news conference to announce that development. Immediately following the news conference, the Iowa attorney general's office and Iowa Division of Criminal Investigation issue a joint statement announcing that they have begun an investigation.

Spring 2012

The money from the jackpot is returned to the lotteries in the Hot Lotto game in proportion to the sales that had come from each jurisdiction.

Summer 2012

The Iowa Lottery gave away its share of the returned jackpot money in a promotion called "Mystery Millionaire," which ran in July and August 2012. Dozens of players won prizes in Mystery Millionaire, including a retired Des Moines police officer who won the promotion's top prize of $1 million during a live finale event on August 20, 2012 at the Iowa State Fair.

October 9, 2014

The DCI releases surveillance-camera video of the man making the Hot Lotto ticket purchase in December 2010. The DCI also states that its investigative information had led agents to pursue additional leads in the Houston area.

January 15, 2015

The DCI and attorney general's office announce that charges have been filed in the case. Eddie Tipton, of Norwalk, Iowa, was arrested and charged with two counts of fraud. Tipton was an employee of the Multi-State Lottery Association (MUSL), an Urbandale, Iowa-based lottery vendor organization that handles the day-to-day functions in multi-state lottery games on behalf of its member lotteries.

March 21, 2015

The DCI and the Iowa attorney general's office announce additional charges in the case. Robert Rhodes, of Sugar Land, Texas, was arrested March 20 and charged with two felony counts of fraud. According to the criminal complaint, Eddie Tipton previously worked for Rhodes' Houston-based company and Rhodes intentionally conspired with others to attempt to influence the winning of a lottery prize.

July 13, 2015

Trial for Eddie Tipton begins in Des Moines.

July 20, 2015

A Polk County District Court jury finds Eddie Tipton guilty of both counts of fraud.

September 9, 2015

Eddie Tipton is sentenced to 10 years in prison, the maximum penalty for the charges. In handing down the sentence, Polk County District Court Judge Jeffrey Farrell said Tipton's crime represented a massive breach of trust.

October 9, 2015

The Iowa attorney general's office files a felony charge of violating Iowa's ongoing criminal conduct statute against Eddie Tipton, stemming from lottery jackpot prizes won in two different games in 2005 in Colorado and 2007 in Wisconsin. The criminal complaint against Tipton states that he helped build the random-number generator equipment used in the jackpot drawings in Colorado and Wisconsin. The complaint further states that according to court testimony earlier this year, Tipton had the technical ability and opportunity to tamper with the drawing equipment that picks the winning lottery numbers in order to make the numbers predictable.

October 12, 2015
The judge in the Eddie Tipton legal proceedings in Polk County District Court approves a request from the Iowa attorney general's office to add a charge of money laundering against Tipton.

October 16, 2015
The Iowa attorney general's office expands the evidence in the ongoing criminal conduct charge against Eddie Tipton to include a jackpot prize claim in 2011 in Oklahoma.

December 21, 2015
Court documents filed in the case by the Iowa attorney general's office again expand the evidence in the ongoing criminal conduct charge against Eddie Tipton to include two jackpot prize claims in 2010 in Kansas.

March 30, 2016
A felony charge of violating Iowa's ongoing criminal conduct statute is filed against Tommy Tipton, of Flatonia, Texas. Tommy Tipton is Eddie Tipton's younger brother and a former justice of the peace in Texas. The criminal complaint against him states that Tommy Tipton aided and abetted in thefts for financial gain. According to the complaint, witnesses would testify that Tommy Tipton chose his own numbers and bought lottery tickets that won a jackpot in 2011 in Oklahoma and a share of a jackpot in 2005 in Colorado, then recruited others to claim the prizes in exchange for a small portion of the money.

June 2016
Trial for Robert Rhodes is scheduled to begin February 27 in Iowa's Polk County District Court.

June 24, 2016

A judge rules that Eddie Tipton's trial on charges of ongoing criminal conduct and money laundering will be moved out of Polk County. According to the judge's order, a new trial date and venue will be chosen at a later date.

July 27, 2016

The Iowa Court of Appeals rules in Eddie Tipton's appeal of his conviction on two fraud charges from his July 2015 trial in Polk County. The court upheld Tipton's conviction for tampering with the equipment used in the Hot Lotto drawing on December 29, 2010 with the intent to influence winnings. For timeliness reasons, the court overturned Tipton's conviction for passing or attempting to redeem a lottery ticket with the intent to defraud. The case was sent back to district court.

August 24, 2016

The Iowa attorney general's office seeks the public's assistance in providing information regarding any relationship between two Texas attorneys— Thad Whisenant of The Woodlands and Luis Vallejo of La Grange—and those charged in the jackpot investigation case. The Iowa state lawyers also seek the court's permission to subpoena bank and telephone records from Vallejo and Whisenant. In its court filings, the attorney general's office indicates that it believes the two men have ties to Tommy Tipton.

December 22, 2016

A second state files charges in the long-running investigation. The Wisconsin Department of Justice files charges against both Eddie Tipton and his long-time friend Robert Rhodes. Tipton faces six charges: racketeering, theft by fraud, and four charges of computer crimes. Rhodes faces two charges: racketeering and theft by fraud. According to the Wisconsin criminal complaint, Rhodes confessed to authorities that Tipton first approached him with the possibility of rigging a lottery drawing and Rhodes ultimately went along with and participated in the scheme.

January 2017

Trial for Eddie Tipton on charges of ongoing criminal conduct and money laundering is delayed until July 10, 2017, with a court location to be determined. Trial for Tommy Tipton, on a charge of ongoing criminal conduct, is delayed until September 11, 2017.

January 9, 2017

During a hearing in Iowa's Polk County District Court, Robert Rhodes II, of Sugar Land, Texas, pleads guilty to a Class D felony charge of lottery fraud. Specifically, he pleaded guilty to violating Iowa Code section 99G.36(2) concerning the use of coercion, fraud, deception, or tampering with lottery equipment in the winning of a prize. The judge at the hearing accepted Rhodes' plea. A sentencing date for Rhodes was not set, with both sides noting the preference to have his cooperation and testimony against Eddie Tipton and Tommy Tipton at their upcoming trials.

February 13, 2017

The Iowa Supreme Court hears arguments in an appeal by Eddie Tipton of his conviction for tampering with the equipment used in the Hot Lotto drawing on December 29, 2010, with the intent to influence winnings. The court will issue its decision at a later date.

March 15, 2017

Kansas Attorney General Derek Schmidt announces he has filed a civil lawsuit against Eddie Tipton and two of his acquaintances, Amy Demoney of Waukee, Iowa and Christopher McCoulskey of Denton, Texas. The suit filed in Kansas' Shawnee County District Court seeks to recoup two prizes of $22,000 they received from redeeming lottery tickets linked to Eddie Tipton. In the lawsuit, Schmidt alleges that in December 2010, Tipton purchased two lottery tickets at convenience stores in Kansas, then gave the tickets to Demoney and McCoulskey to present them for payment to the Kansas Lottery. According to the suit, in February and June of 2011, Demoney and McCoulskey submitted the tickets to the Kansas Lottery and were paid a total of $44,008, then gave a portion of the winnings to Tipton. In addition to seeking repayment for the winnings paid, the lawsuit asks the court to impose civil penalties for violations of the Kansas False Claims Act.

March 27, 2017

Robert Rhodes pleads guilty in Wisconsin to a felony charge of being party to a computer crime. A plea agreement calls for him to serve six months' home confinement in Texas and pay $409,000 in restitution to the state of Wisconsin. Rhodes said in a deposition that his actions were wrong. He agreed to testify against Eddie Tipton.

June 12, 2017

In an agreement with the states of Colorado, Iowa, and Wisconsin, Eddie and Tommy Tipton plead guilty and agree to pay restitution. For his central role in the case, Eddie Tipton pleaded guilty in Iowa to a felony charge of ongoing criminal conduct and in Wisconsin to felony charges of theft by fraud and computer crime. Tommy Tipton pleaded guilty in Iowa to a felony charge of conspiracy to commit theft and in Wisconsin to a misdemeanor count of the same charge. The Tipton brothers also agreed to pay a total of $2.2 million in restitution to the Colorado, Kansas, Oklahoma, and Wisconsin lotteries.

June 23, 2017

The Iowa Supreme Court issues its ruling in Eddie Tipton's appeal from his 2015 trial in Iowa's Polk County. In its ruling, the court determined that the equipment-tampering charge was filed too long after the DCI was put on notice of a potential crime, so that charge could not move forward. However, the court held that the actions by Crawford Shaw in attempting to claim the Hot Lotto jackpot prize were timely enough to allow that portion of the fraud charge against Tipton to move forward. The court ordered a new trial for Tipton. However, with the comprehensive plea deal already reached, the court's ruling had little practical effect.

June 29, 2017

Eddie and Tommy Tipton appear in Iowa's Polk County District Court to enter their pleas as part of the agreement with the three states. For the first time in an Iowa court, Eddie Tipton admitted to writing and installing malicious code on lottery computers that allowed him to predict the winning numbers in some drawings. Eddie Tipton said he then shared the numbers with others to claim lottery prizes. Tommy Tipton admitted that he claimed prizes in Colorado and Oklahoma using numbers that his brother provided to him. After entering his plea, Tommy Tipton was immediately sentenced to 75 days in jail.

August 22, 2017

Eddie Tipton is sentenced in Iowa's Polk County District Court to up to 25 years in prison, the maximum sentence for the felony charge of ongoing criminal conduct to which he pleaded guilty in Iowa. That's what the prosecutor had recommended. Eddie Tipton said he regretted his actions in rigging lottery drawings, that he knew he was wrong, and he expressed remorse for hurting so many people. The judge said the maximum sentence was intended to deter this type of fraud. After the hearing, Tipton, the man who had built a very nice house and the foundation of the strangest lottery fraud in U.S. history, was taken into custody.

August 25, 2017

Robert Rhodes is sentenced in Iowa's Dallas County District Court to two years' probation and six months' home confinement after he pleaded guilty to fraud and computer crime charges in Iowa and Wisconsin.

CAST OF CHARACTERS

Iowa Lottery

Terry Rich, CEO (retired Dec. 31, 2018).

Mary Neubauer, vice president, external relations.

Steve Bogle, vice president, security, 2011–2015.

Rob Porter, vice president, general counsel, 2014–present.

Molly Juffernbruch, general counsel, 2009–2014.

Cam Coppess, vice president, security, 2015–present.

State of Iowa

Rob Sand, assistant attorney general, lead prosecutor, 2015–2018. Elected state auditor November 2018.

Thomas H. Miller, assistant attorney general, lead prosecutor before 2015.

Don Smith, special agent and lead investigator.

Matt Anderson, special agent, lead investigator before Smith.

Multi State Lottery (MUSL)

Chuck Strutt, executive director, 1992–2016.

Bill Miller, outside counsel to board, Dorsey Whitney law firm, Des Moines, Iowa.

Rose Hudson, Louisiana Lottery executive director, MUSL board chairwoman, 2014–2015.

Jeff Anderson, Idaho Lottery executive director, MUSL chairperson, 2015–2016.

Ed Stefan, information technology lead, 2002–2014. Hired friend Eddie Tipton.

Rollo Redburn, Oklahoma Lottery director and MUSL audit

committee chairman.

Gary Grief, Texas Lottery director and MUSL board chairman, 2016–2017.

Bret Toyne, executive director, June 2016–present. Long-time past deputy director through June 2016.

Eddie Tipton, I.T. and security director, 2003-2014. Felon linked to rigged lotteries in five states.

Charlie McIntyre, New Hampshire Lottery director, chair of the Hot Lotto Game and MUSL legal chair, 2013-2015.

Others

Robert C. Rhodes, Tipton friend and business associate, partner in lottery fraud.

Robert L. Sonfield, Rhodes' attorney in Houston.

Philip Johnston, Canada lawyer, president of Belize trust that attempted to cash bogus lotto ticket. Had worked with Sonfield on past stock deals.

Crawford Shaw, New York lawyer who hired Des Moines law firm to help Johnston cash the contested lotto ticket in December 2010. Business partner of Sonfield.

Tommy Tipton, justice of the peace in Flatonia, Texas, Bigfoot hunter, linked to fraudulent lottery claims in Colorado and Texas that also were tied to his brother, Eddie.

J. Thad Whisenant, Houston attorney connected to Luis Vallejo of La Grange, TX, who was suspected of being financially involved on the 2005 Colorado claim.

SOURCES

"A Sugar Land man helped pull off the biggest ever multi-state lottery scam," by Craig Malisow, Houston Press, May 2, 2017.

Author's person observations of "Jerry Springer Show."

"Confessions of a lottery scammer," Jason Clayworth, USA Today, March 26, 2018

"Cover Story: The Notorious Lottery Heist," The Game Show Network, January 28, 2018.

Deposition of MUSL's Charles Strutt, Polk County District Court Criminal Case No. FECR282773, Dec. 9, 2015

"Eddie Tipton sentenced in Iowa Lottery rigging case," Jason Clayworth, Des Moines Register, Aug. 22, 2017 https://www. desmoinesregister.com/story/news/investigations/2017/08/22/iowa-lottery-cheat-sentenced-25-years/566642001/

Excerpts from the Qur'an, Sura 2, Al-Baqarah 2:264 http://bit. ly/2qW1pLV

Feature film, "Mission Impossible," starring Tom Cruise, Paramount Pictures, 1996

"4 lottery scandals that rocked the industry," Nicholas Christensen, Lottery Critic, Dec. 1, 2018 https://www.lotterycritic.com/news/lottery-scams/4-lottery-scandals-that-rocked-the-industry/

Glenn Miller Birthplace Society, glennmiller.org

Greater Des Moines Partnership blog http://bit.ly/2qZjw3E

"Guilty plea in lottery scheme," Associated Press, Oct. 20, 1988 https://
www.nytimes.com/1988/10/20/us/guilty-plea-in-lottery-scheme.html

Iowa Lottery file video, news conference, Jan. 26, 2012

Iowa Lottery statement on Eddie Tipton sentencing, Aug. 22, 2017

"Jackpot-fixing investigation expands to more state lotteries," Ryan
Foley, Associated Press, Dec. 18, 2015

Letter to Julie Johnson McLean, Davis Brown Law, from Molly
Juffernbruch, vice president and general counsel, Iowa Lottery, Jan. 26, 2012

Letter to Molly Juffernbruch, vice president and general counsel Iowa
Lottery, from Julie Johnson McLean, Davis Brown Law, Jan. 25, 2012

Lottery staff archive interviews:
- Terry Rich
- Mary Neubauer
- Rob Sand
- Steve Bogle
- Cam Coppess
- Rob Porter
- Thomas H. Miller

Jackpot investigation timeline, Iowa Lottery

LinkedIn listing, Eddie Tipton

Memorandum, "Completion of Hot Lotto Draw Review," William J.
Miller, Dorsey & Whitney LLP, April 29, 2016. Response from U.S.
Senator John Thune to Multi-State Lottery Association, July 7, 2016

News releases, Iowa Lottery

Proffer of Eddie Tipton, Polk County District Court Case No. FECR289551, June 29, 2017

Proffer of Tommy Tipton, Polk County District Court Case No. FECR294192, June 29, 2017

Terry Rich, former Iowa Lottery CEO author interview, , Aug. 21, 2018, Des Moines, Iowa

Terry Rich, former Iowa Lottery CEO, author interview, Aug. 27, 2018, Des Moines, Iowa

Terry Rich, former Iowa Lottery CEO, author interview, Oct. 5, 2018, Des Moines, Iowa

Terry Rich, former Iowa Lottery CEO, author interview, Oct. 18, 2018, Des Moines, Iowa

Terry Rich, PowerPoint presentation

The Holy Bible, Luke 12:15

Thomas Weber, Gandhi as Disciple and Mentor, Page 227, Cambridge University Press, 2004. CNBC, "$1.5 billion Mega Millions jackpot still unclaimed," November 16, 2018 https://cnb.cx/2QUoM3H

"With hundreds of millions to their names, Iowa Powerball winners leap into demanding jobs," Mike Kilen, the Des Moines Register, Nov. 19, 2018, http://bit.ly/2DxZeG2

"Where the money went," Iowa Lottery Excel spreadsheet

Iowa Lottery recordings of investigative phone calls

Iowa Supreme Court decision, No. 15-1515, State of Iowa v. Eddie
Tipton, filed June 23, 2017
Website, Multi-State Lottery Association, www.musl.com

"Italy hit by lottery scandal," David Wiley, BBC News, Jan. 15, 1999
http://news.bbc.co.uk/2/hi/europe/256206.stm

Lottery Post articles:

2011
- Deadline for claiming $16.5M Hot Lotto jackpot nears, Sept 21, 2011
- Unclaimed Iowa lottery jackpot to expire Dec. 29, Dec. 1, 2011
- Iowa $16.5M Hot Lotto winner claims prize with two hours to spare, Dec. 29, 2011

2012
- Iowa Lottery security chief bent on determining identity of jackpot winner, Jan. 10, 2012
- NY lawyer in lottery mystery travels to Iowa this week, Jan. 17, 2012
- Iowa Lottery security chief to grill NY lawyer over Hot Lotto ticket, Jan. 17, 2012
- Representative of Hot Lotto winner named in lawsuit, Jan. 20, 2012
- Hot Lotto trust representative won't name winner, Jan. 20, 2012
- Iowa Lottery threatens to deny jackpot payout if winner stays anonymous, Jan. 23, 2012

- Lawyer gives up $14 million Iowa lottery ticket claim, Jan. 26, 2012
- $14.3 million Hot Lotto prize claim withdrawn, Jan. 27, 2012
- Iowa Legislators satisfied with Lottery's handling of mystery jackpot winner, Feb. 1, 2012
- Iowa Lottery to give away millions from jackpot mystery, Feb. 26, 2012
- Iowa Lottery director: 50-50 that Hot Lotto mystery will be solved, Aug. 9, 2012
- Iowa officials trying to solve lotto mystery, may release surveillance video, Aug. 19, 2012

2013

- 1 year later, Iowa Lottery still hunting for suspicious no-show winner, Jan. 30, 2013
- Inquiry in Iowa Lottery mystery touches Canada, Jul. 26, 2013
- Lottery jackpot probe heats up after immunity deal, Oct. 8, 2013

2014

- Iowa Lottery still hunting mystery Hot Lotto winner [video], Oct. 10, 2014

2015

- MUSL employee arrested in Hot Lotto jackpot mystery, Jan. 15, 2015
- BOMBSHELL: MUSL employee might have rigged Hot Lotto computerized drawing, Apr. 13, 2015
- Texas man charged in Iowa lottery case contests extradition, Apr. 20, 2015
- Extradition trial begins this week in $16.5M Hot Lotto fraud case, Jun. 7, 2015
- Inside the biggest lottery scam ever, Jul. 7, 2015

- Trial underway in world's biggest lottery fraud case, Jul. 14, 2015
- Lottery security chief: Rigging computerized game "sadly" possible, Jul. 15, 2015
- Prosecution rests in Hot Lotto trial, Jul. 16, 2015
- Defense quickly wraps up in Hot Lotto trial, Jul. 16, 2015
- Hot Lotto case moves to jury for deliberations, Jul. 17, 2015
- Former lottery security employee guilty of rigging $14.3M drawing, Jul. 20, 2015
- MUSL security worker who rigged drawing gets 10 years, Sep. 9, 2015
- HOT LOTTO DRAWING CHEAT CHARGED WITH RIGGING MORE JACKPOTS, Oct. 9, 2015
- Texas authorities had previously investigated brother of lottery cheat, Oct. 14, 2015
- Another $1.2M Hot Lotto jackpot rigged by Tipton, officials say, Nov. 21, 2015
- Jackpot-fixing investigation expands to more state lotteries, Dec. 18, 2015
- Prosecutors say Tipton rigged two jackpots he purchased tickets for in Kansas, Dec. 21, 2015
- Maine gives names of Hot Lotto winners to Iowa team looking into rigging scheme, Dec. 23, 2015
- S.C. Lottery assures public no computerized drawings used in state, Dec. 23, 2015
- Kansas lottery players questioning game's integrity, Dec. 23, 2015
- MUSL CHIEF OUSTED OVER JACKPOT-RIGGING SCANDAL, Dec. 23, 2015
- Lottery scandal unlikely to affect New Mexico, official says, Dec. 26, 2015
- Tipton granted delay in next trial until July, Dec. 29, 2015

2016

- Iowa Lottery CEO Terry Rich to answer lottery player questions live Monday evening, Jan. 11, 2016

- First lawsuit in state lottery-fixing scandal seeks millions, Feb. 4, 2016

- MUSL seeks to dismiss lawsuit over rigged jackpot, Apr. 1, 2016

- Lottery scammer's brother facing criminal charges, Apr. 6, 2016

- Investigators find Tipton's software code to rig computerized lottery drawings, Apr. 7, 2016

- Lottery rigging scandal prompts security audit in South Dakota, Apr. 13, 2016

- Preliminary hearing rescheduled for Tommy Tipton in lottery rigging case, Apr. 22, 2016

- Third suspect surrenders in national lottery rigging scandal, Apr. 28, 2016

- Lottery scam investigation comes to Tennessee, May 11, 2016

- Investigators find another friend of Tipton who cashed rigged lottery prize, May 11, 2016

- Convicted computerized drawing fraudster argues Iowa court appeal, Jun. 16, 2016

- U.S. Senate panel demands info in lottery scandal, Jun. 22, 2016

- Lottery rigging trial to be moved out of Des Moines, Jun. 27, 2016

- Eddie Tipton's new trial delayed until 2017, Jul. 1, 2016

- Iowa court reverses part of Tipton's lottery fraud conviction, Jul. 28, 2016

- Internal investigation concludes Tipton acted alone to rig lottery drawings, Aug. 10, 2016

- Prosecutors say 2 more men may be linked to lottery riggings, Aug. 24, 2016

- Judge: winner's lawsuit in lottery-fixing case can continue, Oct. 13, 2016

- Alleged lottery scandal conspirator to enter new plea, Nov. 14, 2016
- Accused lottery rigger Eddie Tipton facing new Wisconsin charges, Dec. 22, 2016

2017

- Man files lawsuit over rigged lottery jackpots, Jan. 4, 2017
- Trials for Tipton brothers charged in lottery scandal delayed, Jan. 8, 2017
- Former MUSL official received severance amid lottery jackpot scandal, Jan. 10, 2017
- Texas man pleads guilty to fraud in lottery scandal case, Jan. 11, 2017
- Iowa Supreme Court hears lottery rigging case, Feb. 14, 2017
- Kansas files lawsuit against accused lottery rigger, Mar. 16, 2017
- Best friend to testify against Tipton at July lottery rigging trial, Mar. 31, 2017

"People have been chasing Bigfoot for 60 years – Here's how it began," Becky Little, History.com https://www.history.com/news/bigfoot-legend-newspaper

Recorded phone conversation with Billy Conn, Iowa investigators, Nov. 13, 2015

Recorded phone conversation with Kyle Conn, Iowa investigators, Nov. 13, 2015

Recorded phone conversation with Crawford Shaw, Iowa investigators, Dec. 30, 2011

Recorded phone conversations with Philip Johnston, Iowa investigators, Nov. 10, 2011; Dec. 5, 2011; Dec. 6, 2011

Ron Harris biography, Gamblingsites.org, https://www.gamblingsites.org/biographies/ron-harris/

"The Man Who Cracked the Lottery," Reid Forgrave, New York Times Magazine, May 3, 2018. https://www.nytimes.com/interactive/2018/05/03/magazine/money-issue-iowa-lottery-fraud-mystery.html

"2 charged in rigging of lottery," Associated Press, May 4, 1988 http://www.nytimes.com/1988/05/04/us/2-charged-in-rigging-of-lottery.html

Warren County, Iowa, assessor records

"Winners in 3 states to split record Powerball jackpot," USA Today, January 14, 2016 http://bit.ly/2S39mus

"GOOD LEADERSHIP IS EASY IN GOOD TIMES. GREAT AND SUCCESSFUL LEADERSHIP IS JUDGED BY WHAT HAPPENS IN ADVERSE TIMES."

TERRY RICH

ABOUT THE AUTHORS

 **Terry Rich** is the retired president and CEO of the Iowa Lottery and an international keynote speaker and author. During his tenure in the lottery business, he increased sales by over $1 billion. He also served as president of the North American Lottery Association, which is responsible for helping states raise over $80 billion and served on the board of Powerball as its audit chair. Under his leadership, the Iowa Lottery cracked the nation's largest lottery fraud and for those efforts, he received the prestigious international Gambling Compliance Outstanding Achievement Award and the Director's Medallion Award from the Iowa Division of Criminal Investigation. Prior to working at the lottery, he was CEO of the Blank Park Zoo; president and CEO of Rich Heritage Inc., a national marketing and television production company which produced shows for HBO, ESPN and Comcast, among others; and vice president of marketing for Heritage Communications Inc. As an entrepreneur, Terry developed Rich Heritage Inc., along with four other companies including radio station KBBM, US Digital Video, Newsletter Ease, and the World Championship Socker League, LLC. Numerous national media appearances include ABC, NBC, HBO, CBS, 20/20, CNN, CNBC, USA Today and The New York Times; a movie host on Starz!; and as a panel guest on the "Tonight Show." Terry has won numerous entrepreneurial and leadership awards in television production and marketing, has a Bachelor of Science in Speech from Iowa State University, is a Bankers Trust Community Board member, governor emeritus at ISU, a member of the cable TV "Pioneers", was named an American Zoo Association Professional Fellow and is director emeritus of the Blank Park Zoo.

www.terryspeaks.com

 **Perry Beeman** is a veteran multimedia journalist with a career spanning nearly four decades. Beeman's published reports and presentations have appeared in Harvard University's Nieman Reports, in journalism guides produced by Arizona State University's Donald W. Reynolds National Center for Business Journalism, at consulates in China, in the Des Moines Register, USA Today, SEJournal, and the Business Record, and in dsm Magazine and Grinnell Magazine. His award-winning work as long-time investigative reporter at the Des Moines Register included a stint as president of the U.S.-based Society of Environmental Journalists, a professional organization promoting quality coverage of environmental issues. He is managing editor of the Business Record and former editorial director of Grinnell College. Beeman served as a fellow at the Marine Biological Laboratory, the International Reporting Project, Carnegie-Mellon University, the National Press Foundation, as a public policy scholar at the Woodrow Wilson International Center for Journalists, and as a trainer for the International Center for Journalists, the Society of Environmental Journalists and the U.S. State Department in Belize, Mexico, Panama and China. He has received major awards from the Overseas Press Club of America, the Gerald Loeb Awards for Distinguished Business and Financial Journalism, UCLA Anderson School of Management, North American Agricultural Journalists, the Society of American Business Editors and Writers, and the Society of Environmental Journalists. Beeman has a degree in journalism and mass communication from Iowa State University, with a minor in environmental studies.

www.perrybeeman.com

Made in the USA
Middletown, DE
25 May 2019